Gainesville

ALIVE WITH OPPORTUNITY

The Gainesville Area Chamber of Commerce and Community Communications, Inc.
would like to express our gratitude to Shands HealthCare for their leadership
in the development of this book.

Library of Congress Cataloging-in-Publication Data

Carson, Ray, 1955-
   Gainesville—alive with opportunity : featuring the photography of
Ray Carson / text by Marina Blomberg ; profiles by Terry Van Nortwick.—
1st ed.
      p. cm.
   "Produced in cooperation with the Gainesville Area Chamber of Commerce."
   Includes bibliographical references and index.
   ISBN 1-58192-042-3
   1. Gainesville (Fla.)—Civilization. 2. Gainesville
(Fla.)—Pictorial works. 3. Gainesville (Fla.)—Economic conditions.
4. Business enterprises—Florida—Gainesville.   I. Blomberg, Marina,
1951-   . II. Van Nortwick, Terry, 1948-   . III. Title.
   F319.G14 C37 2001
   975.9'79—dc21
                                   2001004058

Gainesville

ALIVE WITH OPPORTUNITY

Featuring the photography of Ray Carson • Text by Marina Blomberg • Corporate Profiles by Terry Van Nortwick

Gainesville
ALIVE WITH OPPORTUNITY

Featuring the Photography of Ray Carson
Text by Marina Blomberg
Corporate Profiles by Terry Van Nortwick

Community Communications, Inc.
Publisher: Ronald P. Beers

Staff for *Gainesville: Alive with Opportunity*

Acquisitions *Henry Beers*
Publisher's Sales Associate *Rickey Heaton*
Editor in Chief *Wendi Lewis*
Managing Editor *Kurt R. Niland*
Profile Editor *Amanda J. Burbank*
Editorial Assistants *Krewe Maynard and Eleanor Planer*
Design Director *Scott Phillips*
Designer *Ramona Davis*
Photo Editors *Kurt R. Niland and Ramona Davis*
Proofreader *Carolyn Phillips*
Production Manager *Jarrod Stiff*
Pre-Press and Separations *DCR Graphics*
National Sales Manager *Keely Smith*
Sales Assistants *Brandon Maddox and Annette Lozier*
Accounting Services *Stephanie Perez*

CCI

Community Communications, Inc.
Montgomery, Alabama

David M. Williamson, Chief Executive Officer
Ronald P. Beers, President
W. David Brown, Chief Operating Officer

TABLE OF CONTENTS

Chapter One: A Heritage of the Arts

Art? Gainesville has it: any medium, any form, any style, any size. Gainesville's liberal and creative environment fosters an eclectic mix of art and culture throughout the city.

Chapter Two: The Eclectic Flavor of Life in Gainesville

Gainesville is full of neighborhoods, each with its own age, character, style, and brand of friendliness.

Chapter Three: A College Town

With thousands of students enrolled at the University of Florida and Santa Fe Community College—and thousands more alumni— Gainesville has become one of the most lively, cultured, and educated cities anywhere in which to live and work.

Chapter Four: Business Diversity

It may be considered a small town, but Gainesville and the surrounding area are home to some big companies. Small businesses thrive in the city as well, enhancing the city's sophisticated economic diversity.

Chapter Five: Have the Time of Your Life

Antiques, art, history, holidays, music, seafood, watermelons. You name it, and there's likely a festival devoted to it in this fun-loving city.

Chapter Six: Mind, Body, and Spirit

The quality of life in any city can be measured against the number of resources devoted to caring for the mind, body, and spirit. With its top-notch colleges, hospitals, and churches, Gainesville is home to a healthy, happy, well-rounded population.

Chapter Seven: Beauty of Life

Enchanting and beautiful, Gainesville's natural wonders captivate residents and visitors alike. Here, you will find a land filled with rich, green forests, clear, cold springs, abundant natural lakes, tangles of wild flora, and precious wildlife.

Chapter Eight: Gainesville's Neighbors

Be it north, south, east, or west, a short drive from Gainesville will take you to world-famous attractions, sleepy forgotten towns, and miles of pristine beaches.

Cover photo and photos on pages 113 and 123 by Ray Carson • Photo on page 133 by Randy Batista/Media Image

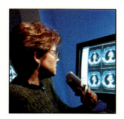

Chapter Nine: Health Care and Education, Quality of Life and Hospitality
Page 98

Chapter Ten: Communications and Energy, Manufacturing and Distribution
Page 114

Chapter Eleven: High Technology
Page 124

Chapter Twelve: Business and Finance
Page 134

Chapter Thirteen: Building Greater Gainesville
Page 148

Chapter One

1

A Heritage of the Arts

Gainesville's museums, theaters, dance companies, and arts organizations set the city's creative climate and provide residents with an opportunity to revel in symphony performances and other live music, ballet and modern dance, plays, and exhibits of fine art. Thanks to the abundance of imagination and expression in Gainesville, even visitors immediately sense the importance and the appreciation of art in this city. *Photo by Ray Carson*

The University of Florida's (UF) Department of Theatre and Dance gives students the opportunity to study with nationally and internationally recognized faculty who are active performers, published scholars, professional designers, and leading educators with a wide range of experiences. Performances are scheduled September through April, and include not only dramatic performances, but more lighthearted fare, particularly by the improvisational group Strike Force, which also performs for schools and organizations. *Photo by Ray Carson*

Dance Alive! is Gainesville's professional dance company. Its repertoire includes modern to traditional, and its annual rendition of "Nutcracker" has been a Gainesville tradition for more than 35 years. Dance instruction is available to all, no matter what their age, expertise, or income. The Gainesville Association for the Creative Arts offers ballet lessons to toddlers and tykes, with scholarships available to those who can't afford the workshops. Dance schools turn out ballerinas and tapdancers who go on to venues such as New York City, Chicago, and Los Angeles. While nationally touring companies regularly visit the Center for the Performing Arts, recitals are also held at UF and Santa Fe Community College as well as the makeshift outdoor stages during the springtime arts festivals. *Photo by Colleen Rand*

(Above) A performance of UF's Department of Theater and Dance. *Photo by Ray Carson*

Many Gainesvilleans are proud to say they started at the "Hipp" (the Hippodrome State Theater) when plays were put on by talented hippies in an abandoned convenience store out Hawthorne Road. The troupe grew professionally when they plied their talents in a corrugated aluminum warehouse in an industrial section north of town. Acquisition of the old post office and its subsequent renovation into a 266-seat main stage and a smaller cinema, art gallery, and bar, has taken years of fund-raising—years marked with some glorious outpourings of monetary support interspersed with occasional panic-stricken brushes with utter failure. The building itself, a fine example of Palladium Classical Revival Architecture, has an interesting history. *Photos by Randy Batista/Media Image*

The Samuel P. Harn Museum of Art is one of the largest university art museums in the southeastern United States. Along with important loans from other sources, the museum's permanent collections feature American, African, pre-Columbian, Asian and other contemporary works of art. It is also home to a real live Monet: *Champ d'avoine* ("Oat Fields"), an 1890 oil painting by the French Impressionist that was donated to the museum by local entrepreneur Mickey Singer, founder of Medical Manager. The museum foundation began gathering collections, several years before the construction of the new building, which opened in the fall of 1990. *Photo by Randy Batista/Media Image*

The Gainesville Community Playhouse offers a more intimate locale to see drama up close. GCP is the oldest community theater in the State of Florida, having been in continuous production since 1927. Each year its season consists of six shows—usually three musicals and three "straight" shows, either dramas or comedies. The present Gainesville Community Playhouse building started out as the Gainesville Woman's Club. It was moved to its present site in northwest Gainesville, next to what is now the Millhopper Shopping Center, more than 35 years ago. A capital campaign is under way to build a new state-of-the-art building. *Photo by Ray Carson*

The Curtis M. Phillips Center for the Performing Arts attracts world-class symphony orchestras, jazz ensembles, comedies, Broadway plays, operas, and large-scale ballet productions. The 1,700-seat main stage theater features a computerized lighting and sound system, a sophisticated fly system for lights and scenery, and an adjustable stage that permits an orchestra pit. The center's 200-seat black box theatre is used for small theater productions, recitals and receptions. The southwest corner of campus, which includes the Phillips Center, the Harn Museum of Art, and the Florida Museum of Natural History, serves as an artistic locale. *Photo by Ray Carson*

The Hippodrome State Theater is a stately, imposing building on the outside, with huge limestone columns rising from granite steps. Inside, it is mirth and melody, tragedy and fantasy, a tight theater-in-the-half-round that has drawn patrons for more than a quarter century. *Photo by Randy Batista/Media Image*

The Thomas Center (below)—originally the home for William Ruben Thomas and his family—became the Hotel Thomas in the 1920s and hosted dignitaries such as Robert Frost and Helen Keller. The hotel closed in 1968 and became a temporary branch campus of Santa Fe Community College. It was crumbling in disrepair when neighbors rallied to save the landmark. It was purchased by the city in 1974, restored, and opened as city offices in 1979. A number of city agencies are housed in the northern buildings, shown in this photo; while the south half is a popular art gallery, musical performance site, and favored wedding and reception location. An outdoor children's theater stage is nestled in the back and the whole grounds serve as one of Gainesville's finest strolling parks and lunchtime retreat for downtown workers. *Photo by Ray Carson*

For many years, the SFCC Spring Arts Festival (above) was the one shot people got at buying fine art off the street. Then came the City of Gainesville's Downtown Festival and Art Show, which celebrates its 20th year in 2001. It began as a simple Artwalk put on by a handful of downtown businesses, and blossomed into a full-fledged cultural event. The weekend of fun begins with a free jazz and blues concert at the Downtown Community Plaza on a Friday night followed by two days of more than 250 artist displays of one-of-a-kind paintings, ceramics, jewelry, photography, and more. Kid's hands-on art projects and food from around the world make it a family event. This festival has been rated in the top 200 best shows in the country by Sunshine Artist magazine, America's premier show and festival publication. *Photo by Kim Bauldree/The Gainesville Sun*

The Fifth Avenue Arts Festival (above and opposite page below) has grown over the past 20 years and now has taken its place as a bonafide draw for 50,000 visitors. While the festival commemorates the historic African-American neighborhood, the music, displays, and food available at the weekend event are an education as well as a revelation of the roots of many Floridians. The festival, which began in 1980 as a forum for organizer Nkwanda Jah to read her poetry, now features a day of motivational speakers, music from gospel to reggae and R&B, dancers and rappers, original artwork, and vendors of food and crafts. *Opposite left photo by John Moran/The Gainesville Sun. This page (above) by John Moran/The Gainesville Sun. (below) by Ray Carson*

■ The 34th Street Wall has become an institution. Once law enforcement personnel gave up trying to prosecute people for decorating long retaining wall along one of the city's busiest thoroughfares, townspeople have taken it upon themselves to assure the wall never appears the same two days in a row. The city even cooperates by placing trash receptacles to hold empty paint cans and used brushes. Memorials are snuggled against war protests, birthday greetings, marriage proposals, party invitations, and declarations of love. Some stuff is silly; some is serious; while often the graffiti is simple spray-can stuff, some others are downright works of art. All of it is worth a drive by every couple of days. *Photo by Randy Batista/Media Image*

■ Art is where you find it. And it is all over the place in Gainesville. A city ordinance requires 10 percent of new construction of public buildings to be devoted to art, be it a sculpture outside or paintings in a public lobby area. Art is also in the eye of the beholder, as exemplified by the 34th Street Wall. Outdoor art, as shown here, is often created from the locally plentiful medium of limestone. *Photo by Randy Batista/Media Image*

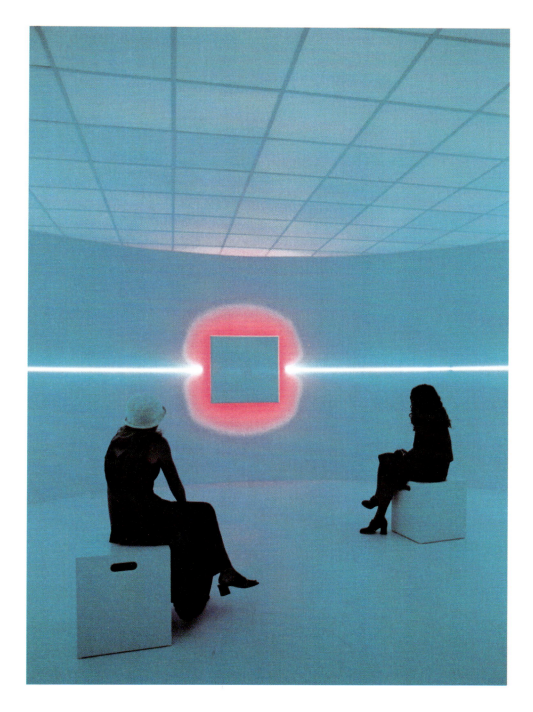

 Art? Gainesville has it: any medium, any form, any style, any size. A liberal and creative environment fosters an eclectic mix of art. Woodcuts and etchings, watercolors and oils, primitive and modern, welded metal sculpture and intricate animals carved from cypress burls, murals that cover the expanse of an interstate overpass and miniature canvases slated for a collector's dollhouse, ceramic or clay, photos or exquisitely detailed quilts—the galleries are full of examples from Gainesville's creative community. The University Gallery on campus showcases students' work, while professionals and amateurs alike display at the Thomas Center, the airport, city hall, and a handful of galleries. A popular event is the occasional art walk through downtown. Galleries and co-ops band together to host a self-guided tour, complete with food and music. Visitors find their way by following brightly painted footprints on the sidewalk. *Photo by Ray Carson: UF News & Public Affairs*

Chapter Two

The Eclectic Flavor of Life in Gainesville

Gainesville is full of neighborhoods, each with its own character, style, and brand of friendliness. The Northeast Historic District, called the Duck Pond Neighborhood, has always been the place for people to renovate, revel in the past, and modernize without changing character. It is a close-knit community of diverse residents—college professors, lawyers, original homeowners, and artists—that is politically powerful as well as historically astute. Home prices run the entire range, from $30,000 starter cottages to those that are in the mid- to upper six figures. *Photo by Ray Carson*

All over town, home-seekers have choices: suburban ranch, South Florida pseudo-Spanish, classic Floridian, postwar bungalow, 1960s modern, Southern Colonial, and some that defy categorization and have evolved from a builder's and a buyer's joint whim. Attached condominiums and cluster housing have just recently been added to the mix.

Some new construction is embracing old ideas: narrow streets, sidewalks, front porches, homes that provide privacy for their families, yet exude a friendly face. Town of Tioga, one such development, is a 500-acre Traditional Neighborhood Development built on the site of an old abandoned settlement. Plans are to have a mix of essential retail, institutional, and recreational uses linked via alley ways, common areas, sidewalks, and bike lanes to facilitate pedestrian activity. The homes are marked by craftsmanship and attention to detail. Gainesville's Pleasant Street District, also known as the 5th Avenue Historic District, is a mere shadow of its former vibrant self. Once a thriving African-American community with shops, businesses, theaters, juke joints, and restaurants, it had declined over the years. But some remnants remain, and increased interest is being shown in protecting and cultivating the buildings with historical significance, while allowing the culture of the neighbors to flow through. *Photos by Ray Carson*

Keifer and Sande Calkin's home (above, left) in the Northeast Historic District is one of the more ornate residences. They "unmuddled" a "muddled" early-1900s restoration to bring the home back to its original Queen Anne splendor. *Photo by Ray Carson*

This three-story Georgian-style home of Carolyn and Hood Roberts (above, right) was previously owned by Senator. W.A. Shands, after whom Shands Hospital is named. Shands, who owned the home from some time in the 1930s to 1952, gutted the house that had been originally built on the property in 1891 and completely rebuilt it. It features high ceilings and hardwood floors. *Photo by Ray Carson*

The Golf View area, nestled between the University of Florida's College of Law and the golf course, is a neighborhood of widely diverse architecture. A home featuring a huge semi-circular glass brick wall surrounding a pool, which is in the front yard, will be right next to a quaint Lilliputian fieldstone house. This home, nicknamed the Turret House, was the home of Jack Harrison, publisher of *The Gainesville Sun* newspaper for many years. Throughout the 1920s and 1930s, new neighborhoods like College Park, Hibiscus Park, and Golf View developed around the University and drew the city westward. *Photo by Ray Carson*

The 2,000-acre Haile Plantation (below) is more than a housing development. It has become a town in itself, with its own walking trails, an 18-hole golf course designed by Gary Player, tennis courts, swimming pools, playgrounds, and a Village Center with over 40 shops and services. More than 3,000 people live there, in two dozen architecturally distinct neighborhoods. The bucolic outer edges belies the activities at the interior. Horses and large garden plots greet guests and residents entering from the east and west.*Photo by Randy Batista/Media Image*

(Opposite page, above) Long hidden from the general populace, which probably led to its intact state, the Haile House was the plantation home of the Haile family. The house was built by Thomas Evans Haile and his wife Serena when they moved to Alachua County in 1854. The house has been virtually unchanged since 1860. It is opened to the public during special fund-raising events. The current Evans Haile is an accomplished pianist, and often plays for the benefits. *Photo by Ray Carson*

(Opposite page, below) Habitat for Humanity is a nonprofit, ecumenical Christian housing ministry. HFH seeks to eliminate poverty housing and hopelessness from the world, and to make decent shelter a matter of conscience and action. Habitat invites people from all walks of life to work together in partnership to help build houses with and for families need. Habitat has built or rehabilitated more than 60,000 houses around the world, providing more than 300,000 people with safe, decent, affordable shelter. The University of Florida and Alachua County co-sponsor Habitat construction. There have been 53 occupied homes, with four under construction in 2001, since 1986. *Photo by Ray Carson*

▣ Alachua County's park facilities keep pace with a variety of sports. When the outdoor roller hockey rink at Kanapaha Park is not filled with battling sticks armed by members of the Gainesville Rollerhockey Academy, it serves as a safe place to learn to roller-blade. *Photo by Randy Batista/Media Image*

▣ Alachua County's Veterans Memorial is more than an edifice to honor fallen heroes, it is a visual living history. Each war from the American Revolution through Vietnam is depicted, and the number of bricks at each station represents the number of Gainesville's fallen soldiers. There is also a monument to police officers killed in the line of duty. This is the newest recreation park in Alachua County, with two playgrounds, two well-maintained soccer fields, two sand volleyball courts, a softball diamond, basketball court, two picnic shelters, and a popular, paved walking trail. *Photo by Randy Batista/Media Image*

A rainbow appears before a gazebo and a tangle of verdant flora at the 62-acre Kanapaha Botanical Gardens. *Photo by Randy Batista/Media Image*

Dogwood Park is a 15-acre private park that allows dogs to run, swim, and explore leash-free. The park also features a dog wash, the Spot Shop (a "doggie boutique"), doggie daycare, and other facilities and services that enhance the quality of life for Gainesville residents and their best friends. *Photo by Randy Batista/Media Image*

Chapter Three

A College Town

UF football game weekends bring literally thousands of people to Gainesville, with alumni and fans from around the state—and the country—streaming in to join townies for a three-hour (or more) ritual at The Swamp, which is the nickname for the Ben Hill Griffin Stadium and Florida field. The stadium is filled to capacity—that's more than 85,461 people—on nearly every home game weekend for the past decade. All these people need to eat, drink, and sleep in town, giving it an economic shot much likened to a long draw of Gatorade after a 5K run. *Photo by Ray Carson: UF News & Public Affairs*

◻ Whether in the classroom or on the field, on campus or off, one doesn't have to look very far to find the iconic Florida gator. Albert and Alberta (right) are UF's main mascots, and a busy couple they are. They make more than 800 appearances every year at football, basketball, and baseball games, as well as charity events, elementary school visits, and a multitude of miscellaneous events. The group donning the mascot uniform is made up of fewer than a dozen individuals: Four to six men standing at least 5' 10" and three to four women no taller than 5' 4". They must be in good physical shape and prepared for the intense heat inside the heavy and warm suit, especially during spring sports. They must be outgoing as well, because they get petted and hugged a lot by kids.

Although not as cute but just as venerated is the gator (below, left) who welcomes UF football fans to "The Swamp," or Ben Hill Griffin Stadium as it is formally known.

Just a little spark of the powerful adult he'll soon be, (below, right) an alligator emerges from its shell at a UF biology lab.
Photos by Ray Carson: UF News & Public Affairs

The University of Florida has 23 colleges and schools and more than 100 research, service and education centers, bureaus, and institutes. More than 100 undergraduate majors are offered. The graduate school coordinates almost 200 graduate programs. Professional degree programs include dentistry, law, medicine, pharmacy, and veterinary medicine. *Photo by Ray Carson: UF News & Public Affairs*

The University Auditorium was completed in the mid-1920s and then renovated and expanded as a bicentennial project in 1976. It is one of several university buildings included in the National Register of Historic Places. The auditorium provides a concert stage, seating for nearly 870 people, and is used for musical concerts, special lectures, convocations, and less-technically demanding dance programs and pageants. The auditorium is also home to the Anderson Memorial Organ. Donated in 1925, the organ has since been expanded and improved with the installation of additional pipes and a state-of-the-art five-manual console, the Southeast. The interior of the building is decorated with fanciful, carved wooden gargoyles. *Photo by Ray Carson: UF News & Public Affairs*

A contemporary steel sculpture created by Florida artist John Henry and named *Alachua* was installed in 1989 at the University of Florida's central science library and computer science/engineering complex. The committee that chose it claimed it embodied the energy and the technological image needed for the building to which it was related. It also expresses some of the cantilever techniques users of the buildings are familiar with and would appreciate. *Photo by Ray Carson: UF News & Public Affairs*

Excluding auditorium classrooms, most UF classrooms are limited in size to under 30—a fact that students must face the beginning of each semester as they hurry to get into needed classes before they are filled. Other courses, by their popularity, are taught via television. While this may be considered a "cold" way to teach, (44 studies and 21 research summaries from 1954 through 1992, encompassing more than 800 separate studies of all levels of instruction from elementary through graduate education to the military) studies show "no significant difference" in terms of students' learning between video-mediated classes and a "traditional" classroom. *Photo by Ray Carson: UF News & Public Affairs*

The Baughman Meditation Center is a crown jewel along UF's Lake Alice. Designed and constructed by private donations, its presence graces the moss-covered oaks and tranquil walking paths in an increasingly busy campus. The building is positioned precisely to flood with light upon the rising and setting of the summer solstice sun. The exterior is clad in tri-colored reflective glass, framed by cypress and copper. The 1,500-square-foot structure has fixed bench seating that accommodates nearly 100 people. While the exterior walls are made of natural Florida cypress and the roof is yellow pine, the interior is structural steel and stained pine planking. The marble floor is made of three shades of travertine marble arranged in a geometric pattern based on the building's structure, reminiscent of the old cathedrals. The center is a perfect place for quiet meditation, as well as weddings and special services. *Photo by Ray Carson: UF News & Public Affairs*

(Opposite page) Originally called North Dormitory, Fletcher Hall was completed in 1939 with assistance of Depression-era programs such as the Works Progress Administration. In 1972, it became co-ed by floors, and a $4 million renovation brought air conditioning—finally!—in 1984. The Collegiate Gothic style residence hall, now housing mostly first-year students, was placed on the National Register of Historic Places in 1989. *Photo by Ray Carson: UF News & Public Affairs*

The University of Florida's Fredric G. Levin College of Law is one of the nation's most comprehensive public law schools. Founded in 1909, the college is accredited by the American Bar Association and is a member of the Association of American Law Schools. Alumni of the college are leaders in law, business, government, and education at the state and national levels. No other law school has produced as many presidents of the American Bar Association in the past 20 years. *Photo by Ray Carson: UF News & Public Affairs*

◻ Coach Steve Spurrier dubbed Ben Hill Griffin Stadium at Florida Field "The Swamp" in 1991 because "The swamp is where Gators live. We feel comfortable there, but we hope our opponents feel tentative. A swamp is hot and sticky and can be dangerous." It is now the largest stadium in the state of Florida (and one of the loudest anywhere in the country). The original football stadium, the lower half of the current facility, was constructed in 1930. The completion of the South End Zone project in August of 1982 raised the seating capacity to over 72,000. The addition of the North End Zone (shown in this photo) brought the capacity over 84,000 seats. Another nearly 2,000 fans people the stadium in various capacities during most games. This end of the stadium also includes the Touchdown Terrace, which not only provides high-priced, indoor seating for football fans, but also a popular site for receptions and meetings. Forty-six skyboxes are settled atop the western edge of the bowl.

With its stellar fireworks display, homecoming festivities, marching band, student skits, videos, and comedian keynote speakers, Gator Growl is billed as the world's largest student-produced pep rally.
Photos by Ray Carson: UF News & Public Affairs

The 157-foot-tall Century Tower was built in 1953-56 to commemorate the 100th anniversary of the founding of the University of Florida's parent institution, Kingsbury Academy in Ocala, and was dedicated to the UF students killed in World Wars I and II. The interior was originally planned as a history museum and art gallery but it was never completed. In 1979, a cast-bell carillon was installed in the Century Tower. There are fewer than 200 of such carillons in all of North America, and only four in Florida. The clock-strike melody is heard progressively on the quarter hours. Through addition and variation, the sequence grows until the complete melody is played just before the hourly toll. Concerts are played on football and Commencement Saturdays and during other campus festive days. *Photo by Ray Carson*

A majority of University of Florida's public events are presented in the O'Connell Center, nicknamed the O-dome. Construction began in the fall of 1977, and the building was completed over three years later. The total cost of the project was $15.9 million, which was paid by student fees earmarked by the Board of Regents and the Legislature for capital improvements that had accumulated over several generations of students. The building itself covers 3.6 acres, or approximately 296,000 square feet. Besides the basketball games, gymnastics meets, concerts, circuses, and crafts festivals that routinely take place inside, there are facilities for recreational swimming in the two Olympic-size pools (one indoors, one out), martial arts, weight-lifting, and other activities. More than a thousand people can participate simultaneously in at least nine different sports inside, not counting the main arena, which seats 12,000 spectators, 8,400 of them in armchairs. Separate bleachers accommodate up to 1,200 people for viewing swimming events. Originally, the building featured a translucent roof, made of Teflon-coated Fiberglass and kept inflated by huge fans that boosted the air pressure in the main arena. During the summer of 1998, the O'Connell Center underwent a major renovation, replacing the air-supported roof with a permanent, steel roof. The new roof is 118 feet above the main arena floor. The building's namesake, Stephen C. O'Connell, a former UF president, died in April 2001. *Photo by Ray Carson: UF News & Public Affairs*

Good season or not, the acrobatic and athletic cheerleaders are always ready to spur the team and its fans on. UF's non-competitive, co-ed varsity squad is comprised of 14 members and cheers at both home and away Gator football games and at men's home basketball games. Members are selected from approximately 60 men and women who try out every year. UF's co-ed Junior Varsity squad, also non-competitive, is made up of 14 members who participate in cheering for all home football games, home volleyball matches, and home women's basketball games. In addition to practice and other on-campus activities and games, the cheerleaders appear at numerous activities around the community. *Photo by Ray Carson: UF News & Public Affairs*

■ UF's intercollegiate athletic programs run whole spectrum of sports competition. For the last decade, UF has ranked among the nation's top five athletic programs. For an unprecedented fourth time, Florida completed a sweep of the Southeastern Conference All-Sports Trophies, winning the men's, women's and combined crowns in 1998. Florida became the first school in SEC (Southeastern Conference) history to win all three in 1992 and has since repeated the feat in 1993, 1996, and 1998. Also in 1997-98, a league record 100 student-athletes were named to the SEC's Academic Honor Roll. *Left Photo by Ray Carson. Photo below by Jeff Gage*

◾ While UF seems to grab most of the headlines, Santa Fe Community College can hardly be overlooked among Gainesville's educational facilities. With 12,500 students enrolled, it hefts its own weight around the community. Courses include liberal arts and sciences, business, health, agriculture, engineering, and technology. Graduates in the popular graphic design programs have a 90 percent hire rate. *Photos by Ray Carson*

◾ Santa Fe's Zoo Animal Technology Program is a five-semester technical program that offers a wide range of instruction and clinical experiences leading to the Associate Science Degree in Zoo Animal Technology. A teaching zoo on campus features such diverse animals as the Burmese brown tortoises, the largest Asiatic tortoise, growing to lengths of over 24 inches, and a variety of exotic snakes, including two ball pythons. This docile reptile earned its name because when it is disturbed it will coil up into a ball and place its head down in the center. The zoo is open to the public, with several well-attended open houses during the year. A "Boo at the Zoo" celebration during Halloween is a real hoot. *Photos by Ray Carson*

4

Chapter Four

Business Diversity

Gainesville provides a unique environment for business growth and development, encouraging a diversity of size and scope. The presence of one of the nation's premier universities—University of Florida—creates a climate of knowledge and growth that benefits a ready workforce and provides for state-of-the-art technology and facilities. Several forces—city and county governments, the University of Florida, and the U.S. Department of Commerce— have partnered to invest nearly $1 million in a 30,000-square-foot Technology Enterprise Center of Gainesville/Alachua County. This "technology incubator" will house as many as thirteen startup companies for a maximum of three years, until they can operate on their own. This new technology incubator will join the existing UF Sid Martin Biotechnology Incubator in giving Gainesville an enviable status as the place to do business in the growing market-place of the "new economy." *Photo by Ray Carson*

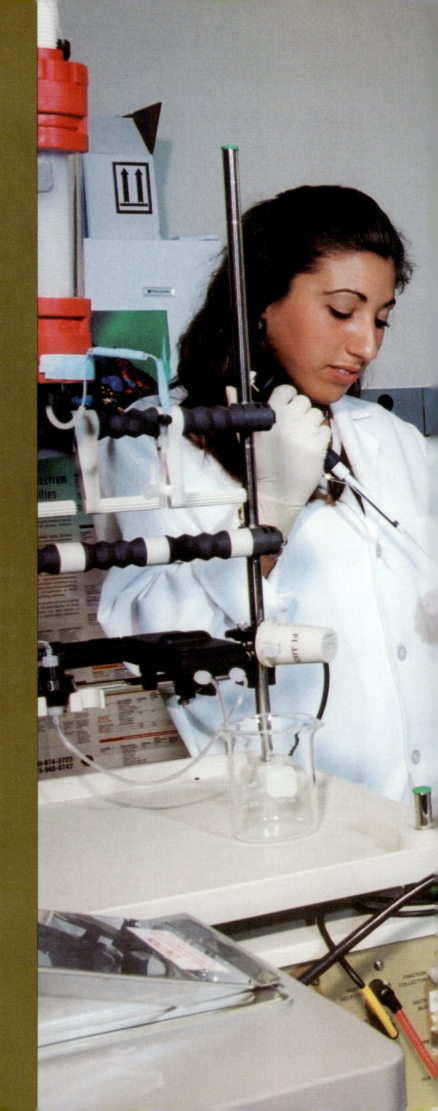

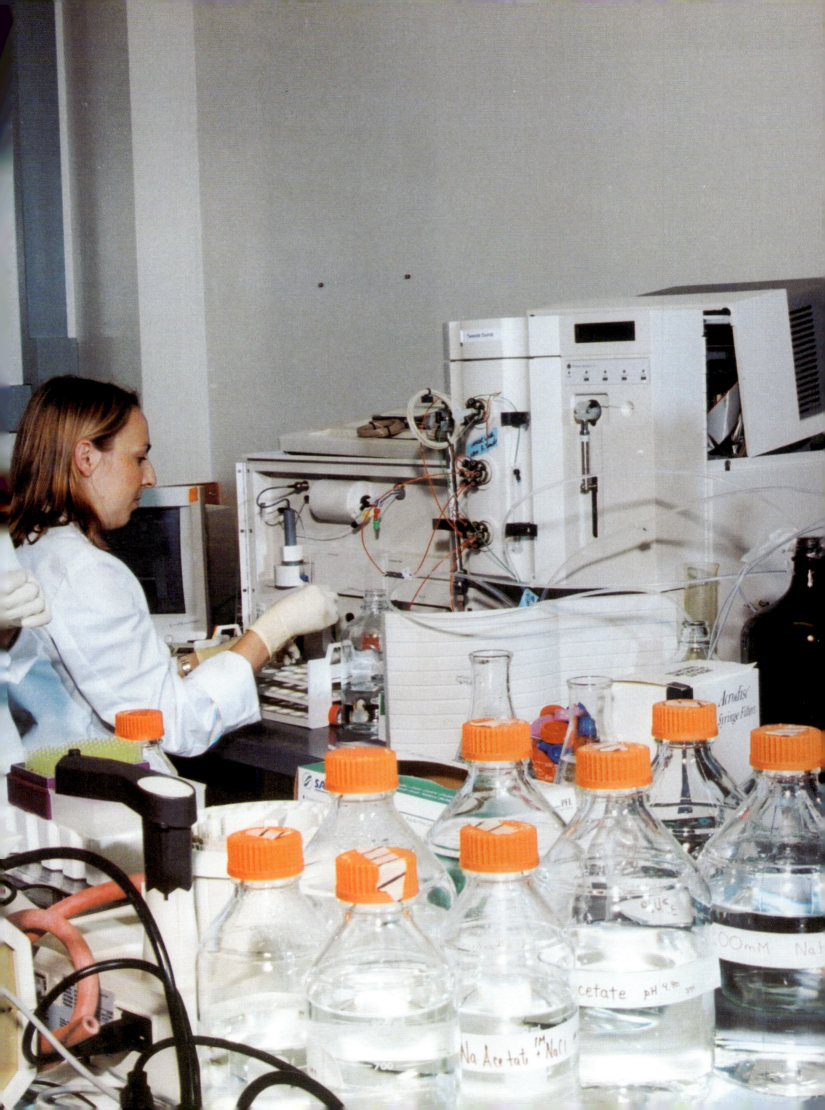

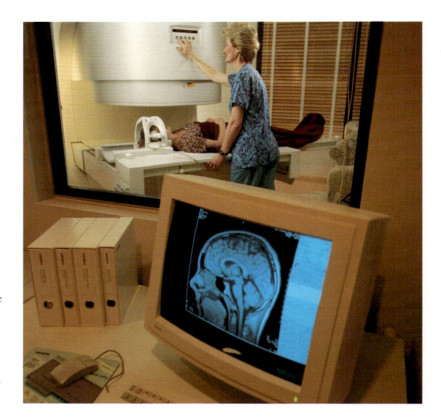

■ Medical technology and biotechnology form a sector of Gainesville's economy that is continually growing to keep pace with global healthcare needs. At left, an Exactech employee inspects hip replacement parts at the company's Gainesville facilities. UF's Sid Martin Biotechnology Incubator (below right) helps biotech startups through all stages of business growth while providing top-notch facilities for research and development. *Right and below left by Randy Batista/Media Image. Below right by Ray Carson*

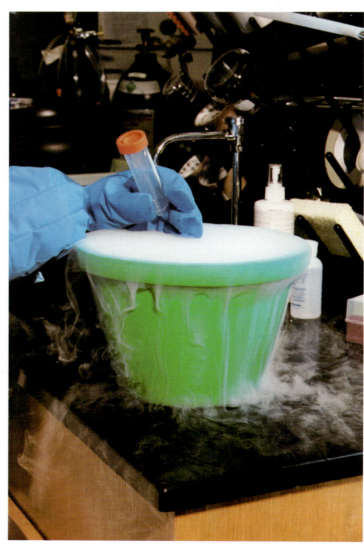

While many dot-coms elsewhere begin to unravel at the motherboard, technological business continue to successfully weave their magic in Gainesville. The hometown Atlantic.Net, founded by two UF students in 1994, now has about 80 workers and 50,000 customers, both business and consumers. e.builder, an internet company that provides software for construction companies, and Medical Manager, the highly successful company that developed software for doctors to run their practices, are two locally based companies that continue to grow. Pictured here is the headquarters of Barr Systems. *Photo by Randy Batista/Media Image*

The southwest gateway to Gainesville, with a heavily traveled four-lane Archer Road/State Road 24 making a beeline between Interstate 75 and the University of Florida campus and attendant hospitals, has become a shopper's heaven. Three large shopping centers—West, Central, and East— are strung along the "Miracle Mile," all owned by Clark Butler Enterprises. The site was a former World War II airfield. Student housing is plentiful, and fast-food restaurants line the curbs. Businesses range from Target at one end to Lowe's Home Improvement on the other, with groceries, discount stores, office suppliers and clothing stores in between. *Photo by Ray Carson*

The construction of the Oaks Mall in 1978, and its doubling in size just two years later, created a volcanic change in the town's shopping habits, the reverberations of which are still felt today A major renovation in recent years has upgraded the single-story mall's interior. There are approximately 150 shops, restaurants, vendors, and service outlets. The mall's spacious interior is also a high-traffic venue for new car displays, antique exhibits, and various plant shows and community fund-raisers. Its empty halls are also a popular early-morning walk for senior citizens. It's nearly a mile all the way around. *Photo by Ray Carson*

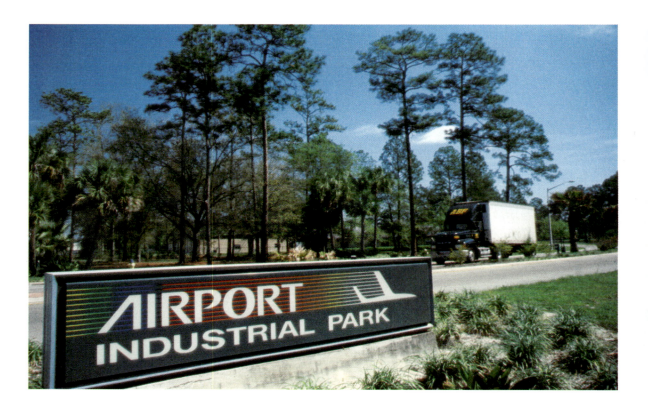

It may be considered a small town, but Gainesville and Alachua County are home to big companies. For the three Nordstrom stores in the Southeast, including the Mall of Georgia store in Buford, Gainesville's new distribution center in the Airport Industrial Park (right) plays an important part in making sure shoes as well as other merchandise get to the floor. The 185,000-square-foot facility opened last year and employs 52 people. It serves three Nordstrom stores in the Atlanta area and will serve additional stores in Florida and Georgia as the company expands. Hunter Marine builds its popular sailing yachts here—almost an anomaly since it's 50 miles to the nearest salt water, but the plant is only a few miles from I-75, which links it to sailors all over the country. That is also the reason that the Dollar General corporation built a 1.2-million-square-foot distribution center near Alachua. Regeneration Technologies, the world's second largest processor of human tissue, is also building an 110,000-square-foot headquarters. Gainesville is also home to the regional Nationwide Insurance office, with 1,050 employees; and North American Archery Group, the international supplier of power bows and archery equipment. The industrial park originally was a gift from the federal government, which had used the property as a training base during World War II. In the 1940s, the federal government gave it to the city to use as an industrial park, a common practice after the war. Today, the industrial park houses nine companies that employ more than 800 people. Overall, the park generates about $1.2 million in annual property taxes. *Photo courtesy of Dollar General. Photo below by Ray Carson*

While it's usually easy to book a hotel room in town, there are more than a dozen times each year when you can't find a single room vacant: home football games; the main graduation weekends; and the spring weekend when the NHRA Gatornationals are in town. Extended-stay motels are convenient for those doing business with the university and the main hospitals. A Sheraton, two Holiday Inns, and a Residence Inn located near UF remain full. And then there are the mom-and-pop motels along SW 13th Street catering to UF visitors and businessmen, and the bed-and-breakfasts, which are becoming increasingly popular not only with out-of-town visitors, but with locals who want to get away—but not too far away—for a night. The new $35-million UF Doubletree Hotel and Conference Center has added a new and refined place for weekend visitors as well as conventions. *Photo by Ray Carson*

Magnolia Plantation—formerly the Baird Mansion, built in 1885—is a bed-and-breakfast just seven blocks from the center of town at the edge of the Southeast Historic District. Joe and Cindy Montalto offer Victorian romance with Southern hospitality. The airy French provincial home features fourteen rooms, eight of them overnight accommodations. (Be sure to try to try the Magnolia Room, formerly the master suite on the corner of the second floor, which includes a separate bathroom and a claw-foot tub.) The grounds are lushly landscaped and include a water pond. The building, while nearly destroyed by years of student tenants, was lovingly restored in the mid 1980s. Several nearby homes have likewise been transformed into bed-and-breakfasts and upper-scale apartments. *Photo by Ray Carson*

The brick and stucco Alachua County Courthouse, right, is one of the larger structures in the downtown complex of government and judicial buildings. While it was built only about 20 years ago, the county's growth has required it to acquire more property and build a new courthouse nearby to handle the number of legal and judicial activities. The new criminal courthouse will essentially double the amount of space available for county court matters. The existing courthouse has about 101,000 square feet and is expected to continue to house civil court proceedings.

Of the more than 75,400 jobs available in Alachua County, 39,598 are government. Most of those are at UF, but the city of Gainesville employs slightly more than 2,000 workers, with an additional 750 at Gainesville Regional Utilities, the central office of which is shown at right. *Photo by Randy Batista/ Media Image*

Gainesville's four-story main city hall building, built in the late 1960s, now houses city offices and the main commission meeting room, which was moved from the fourth floor to the more accessible ground floor in 1995. The former Alachua County Library District building next door, vacated when the library moved into spacious new quarters across the street, was renovated and includes the city's management, human resources, and economic development agencies. The grounds of the complex include koi ponds and a rose garden as well as a clock tower, which incorporates the original Alachua County clock rebuilt by horologist Ted Crom in a tower built to mirror the old 1900s courthouse pergola. *Photo by Randy Batista/Media Image*

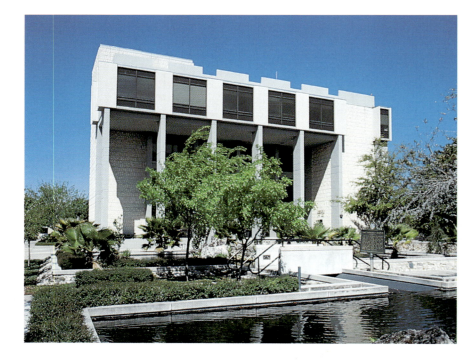

▣ The Gainesville Sun, a daily newspaper with a circulation over 60,000, reports news and events for a 10-county area of North Central Florida. It celebrates its 125th anniversary in 2001. The Sun spearheaded a local Celebrate 2000 campaign, which promoted civic and community events held to commemorate the turning of the millennium. *Photo courtesy of **The Gainesville Sun***

▣ An active member in its community, Cox Communications (below) was named Alachua County Business Partner of the Year 2000 by Florida's Education Commissioner for its work with Alachua County Schools. It is also the sponsor of the Gainesville Area Chamber of Commerce Leadership Gainesville program for 1999 and 2000, which helps 35 local residents enhance their leadership abilities and prepares them for active roles within their community. *Photo by Ray Carson*

◻ With its burgeoning multicultural population, Gainesville is rich in variety when it comes to cuisine. There isn't a culture that isn't represented by the local restaurants, groceries, and specialty shops. Bakeries such as Upper Crust (pictured here) cater to those whose taste buds require freshness and something different from supermarket fare. And the international flavor of the town isn't just at the dinner table: clothing, music, art, and books are offered at specialty shops all over town. *Photo by Randy Batista/Media Image*

◻ (Opposite) Gainesville is surrounded by farm country. While the University of Florida is a national leader in agricultural research and technology, there are more than 1,000 people actively involved in the business of farming, fishing, and raising trees in the Alachua County area. Watermelons, hay, corn, cattle, horses, and major landscape nurseries make up a large comfy agrarian quilt wrapped around the technical and educational center of town.

Locally, small growers are finding a ready market for their fresh produce at five active open-air farmers markets. And there is an active movement toward sustainable agriculture, with organic farming, holistic poultry farms, and herb greenhouses filling necessary niches. *Photo by Ray Carson*

5

Chapter Five

Have the Time of Your Life

The Alachua County Fair, featuring carnival rides, games of skill, and an array of sticky, flavorful food, covers several acres of grassy field by the Gainesville airport each November. The Gainesville Jaycees operated the annual event for many years as a fund-raiser. An independent board now organizes it. Besides the midway, the Agricultural Center houses entries in the food, horticulture, and handicrafts competitions. The fair runs for about 10 days, with at least one night designated as "Midnight Madness," where fair-goers can ride all they want for one admission ticket. *Photo by Ray Carson*

◉ For many, Labor Day is truly a day of rest and reflection on the waning of the year. The Annual Fourth of July Fanfare and Fireworks on the University of Florida campus is a brilliant display of festival pyrotechnics with more than 1,000 aerial shells blasting skyward for 30 minutes to the oohs and aahs of the young and old gathered at the shore of Lake Alice. *Photo by The Gainesville Sun*

◉ (Opposite page, above) Being able to supply sweltering Chicagoans with a crisp, juicy Fourth of July melon is the source of pride for many farmers in the western Alachua County and eastern Gilchrist and Levy county areas. Melon farming is not without risk, however, with late freezes and spring droughts wreaking havoc on every year's crop. As much a harvest festival as simply a fun summer fling, both Newberry and Chiefland host watermelon festivals in June. Queen pageants, parades, seed-spitting contests, and free slices of the juicy red fruit (actually a squash, but who's quibbling?) are a welcome respite during our sultry summers. *Photo by The Gainesville Sun*

◉ (Opposite page, below) The Alachua Music Harvest Festival is a three-day rock-n-roll party that draws more than 20,000 people to hear—and dance to—up to 100 different acts on several stages set up at the Alachua County Fairgrounds. Years before they became famous, Sister Hazel and House of Dreams would join garage bands and groups representing the Gainesville nightclub music scene to create a mini-Woodstock. For several years it was held in the fall, but competition with football games and the area's other autumn festivals moved it to spring. It is organized by Gainesville Alternative Music Alliance, now called GAMA Productions, to include areas outside the city. *Photo by The Gainesville Sun*

▣ Micanopy is the second oldest white inland settlement in Florida and was an important Indian outpost before then. Ironically, Micanopy is the sort of place Walt Disney must have had in mind when he came up with "Main Street USA," the archetypal small town at the heart of his parks. It's simple, slow moving and restful, where people still walk to church and school and shopkeepers live close to their businesses. (You may recognize its street and rustic buildings as the site where "Doc Hollywood" starring Michael J. Fox was filmed in 1991. Many locals also appeared in that movie.) The town's old-timey charm attracts many thousands of visitors each year, mostly on weekends. They come to browse the antique shops and artists' galleries, and to enjoy a cool soda or a creamy sundae at one of the bistros. The annual Micanopy Fall Harvest Festival features more than 240 booths stretching from one end of Micanopy's main drag, Cholokka Boulevard, to the other with art, crafts, antiques, clothing, food, and all kinds of other stuff up for perusal and/or purchase. *Photo by Lee Ferinden/Special to* ***The Gainesville Sun***

▣ McIntosh is a community roughly midway between Ocala and Gainesville, but a visit there is a trip back in time, as many of the homes are restored turn-of-the-twentieth-century vintage. To commemorate its past as an important citrus supplier to the rest of the country—as well as being a popular railroad stop for travelers—an 1890s Festival is held each October. It began as a small-town fundraiser to save and restore the little train depot, which was eventually moved a dozen yards off the railroad right-of-way and now houses the town's museum. The festival has since turned into a huge craft fair with music, entertainment, and tours through many of the meticulously kept homes, businesses, and churches. Townspeople also use the occasion to don period clothing and stroll through the tree-shaded lanes. *Photo by Kim Bauldree/The Gainesville Sun*

▣ Since 1974, Gainesville's Spring Pilgrimage has become a venerable tradition to Gainesvilleans. Each year, at the precise moment that the azaleas and dogwoods are at their most splendid, select residents of the Duck Pond area just northeast of downtown open up their restored homes to tours. Visitors are given a glimpse of homes that have withstood not only the test of time—many of the homes in this neighborhood date to the early 1900s, and even earlier—but also the refreshing change of intricate restoration. *Photo by Ray Carson*

There is no scarcity of art festivals and special events that celebrate the arts, with festivals during nearly every month of the year. Spring starts with the Santa Fe Community College Spring Arts Festival, a large celebration that began with a few art classes exhibiting their work on the lawn of the former campus downtown and is now a two-day display of every sort of art imaginable lined along scenic NE 1st Boulevard. Another, even larger, Downtown Arts Festival is held in November, and closes off the Southeast section of downtown. Arts festivals are also held in Cedar Key and Keystone Heights, in the spring and on Labor Day, respectively. The Fifth Avenue Arts Festival has grown over the last 20 years, and now has taken its place as a bona fide draw for Florida visitors. While the festival commemorates the historic African-American neighborhood, the music, displays, and food available at the weekend event are as diverse as all of Gainesville is. *Photos by Ray Carson*

◧ Since its inception in 1969, the Cedar Key Seafood Festival has drawn the hungry from far and wide to sample fried fish dinners, steamed clams, and delectable corn-on-the cob, all cooked and served outdoors along the beachfront of this island community. Even Florida's 1995 net ban, which was feared to curtail the supply of mullet, didn't curb the supply of fresh seafood after all. The town of 791 people welcomes visitors for a weekend of munching and mingling, kicking back and relaxing in the Gulfside sun. *Photo by Matt May/ The Gainesville Sun*

◧ (Opposite page, above) The Gainesville Garden Club hosts a Holiday Tour of Homes each December in which up to a half a dozen homes are decorated by club subgroups called "circles." While the clubwomen do much of the decorating, they often follow the homeowner's theme. The Chuck Perry home featured almost a dozen decorated trees the family normally displays. *Photo by Kim Bauldree/ The Gainesville Sun*

◧ (Opposite page, below) The Holiday Tour of Homes includes several houses within walking distance of each other, so visitors can stroll to each one rather than driving. A garden club bazaar is set up at one of the locations, where people can purchase the decorations they see in several of the homes. This home is an example of the stylish buildings surrounding the University of Florida. *Photo by The Gainesville Sun*

About 140,000 people come to Gainesville each spring—traditionally around St. Patrick's Day—for Gatornationals, a four-day, drag racing event sponsored by the National Hot Rod Association. The cars race down a straight quarter-mile stretch and are clocked for time and speed. At Gainesville Raceway, just north of town, the fastest drivers approach speeds of 330 miles per hour—and at some local businesses, merchants watch their own numbers rise at similar rates. Tourism officials estimate that Gatornationals creates between $25 million and $30 million in economic activity in one week alone. The race is the NHRA's second-highest-attended event, just behind an annual competition in Indianapolis. *Photo by Ray Carson*

(Opposite Page) Civil War re-enactors find many opportunities to practice their avocation. The largest gathering in this part of the state is the re-enactment of the Battle of Olustee each spring. This battle, which took place in February 1864 near Ocean Pond, was the largest Civil War battle in Florida, and, proportionally, the bloodiest: 1,861 Union and 946 Confederate soldiers died. It essentially ended the Union's campaign in the south. Today, the week-long Olustee festival draws 50,000 visitors to the piney woods of the Osceola National Forest between Lake City and Baldwin. *Photos by Ray Carson*

Chapter Six

Mind, Body, and Spirit

Quality of life in any community is connected to the enrichment of the mind, body, and spirit. Together, Gainesville's natural environment, its places of worship, schools and universities, hospitals and clinics, and community resources sustain the highest quality of living possible for its residents. *Photo by Ray Carson*

◻ The chef at your favorite restaurant could very well have been a graduate of Eastside High School Culinary Arts Institute, a high school vocational curriculum focusing on commercial food preparation, but training its students about varied career opportunities and finesse in the kitchen. It is taught in conjunction with The Hungry Ram (EHS mascot is the Ram) is a restaurant operated by the students that is open to the teachers, staff and public. Students operate the restaurant and bakery in order to learn procedures, techniques and skills in food service. Students have two hours a day of on-the-job training in a well-equipped commercial kitchen. Second-semester students accomplish dining-room -operation skills by waiting on tables, being a host/hostess and cashiering. The restaurant menu is determined by the curriculum; each week a different menu is offered as the students rotate through stations. Second-year students become sous chefs and learn kitchen management. The students also run a very popular catering service is part of the vocational training , allowing them to learn advanced skills and techniques while working in the community. Ice carving is a favorite class. *Photo by Ray Carson*

◻ Education doesn't end at high school, community college or even the university. Adult education classes (below) are filled to the brim all year through Santa Fe Community College's Continuing Education classes. Offered three times a year, the courses are thoroughly diverse: from fly-tying to composting, computer code-writing to learning how to practice yoga. *Photo by Ray Carson*

The ACCENT Speaker's Bureau, a function of UF's Student Government, brings national and even international leaders to Gainesville to speak. The events routinely pack the O'Connell Center, University Auditorium, the North Lawn, or anywhere they are held, with not only students—many of whom take advantage of the visitors' views for a class writing assignment—but with the Gainesville public, always eager to stay informed. ACCENT speakers and their subjects are diverse; recent lecturers have included Presidential hopefuls Ross Perot and Bob Dole; former Soviet leader Mikhail Gorbachev; Sister Helen Prejean, author of *Dead Man Walking*; Bob Woodward, a Pulitzer Prize-winning journalist who was one of two writers responsible for reporting the Watergate scandal; William B. Davis, better known as "Cancer Man" on the hit TV series *The X-Files*, and Eduardo Sanchez and Dan Myrick, the writing and directing team of *The Blair Witch Project*. The UF College of Business Administration also brings prominent speakers to campus. Warren Buffett (below) considered the world's greatest stock market investor, recently spoke about his success and his strategies to a group of professors and students. *Photos by Ray Carson*

The 12th annual *U.S. News & World Report* guide to "America's Best Hospitals" ranked the 600-plus-bed Shands at the University of Florida among America's top medical institutions. Hospital specialties include cardiovascular medicine, cancer treatment, neurological services, and organ transplantation. As the major teaching and referral center in the Southeast, Shands also offers a variety of other services including a regional burn center, hyperbaric medicine, and many others, including the 210,000-square-foot Evelyn F. and William L. McKnight Brain Institute of the University of Florida, the center of all brain and spinal cord research on the UF campus. About 300 UF researchers from 50 academic departments and 10 colleges, together with collaborators at more than 75 universities and research institutes around the world, pool their talents to make important discoveries about the brain and transfer them to the patient. The Shands family now embraces a number of local hospitals in North Florida between Gainesville, Lake City, and Jacksonville. *Photo by Randy Batista/Media Image*

SHANDS HEALTHCARE

Shands HealthCare is a not-for-profit health system affiliated with the University of Florida. Founded to care for patients, advance medical knowledge, train healthcare professionals, and help build healthier communities, Shands HealthCare connects service and science in an academic environment. At its heart is the UF Health Science Center, the focus for education and research that drives the services provided throughout Shands. The Shands system in Gainesville includes Shands at the University of Florida, Shands Children's Hospital, Shands at AGH, and two specialty hospitals. In addition, Shands has three rural community hospitals in surrounding counties and an academic medical center in Jacksonville.

There's no question about the quality of health care available in Gainesville, with four major hospitals, and one of those a university teaching and research center. And it is available also to those who may not be able to afford it. We Care, a program administered by the Alachua County Medical Society, has successfully provided specialty medical care and inpatient services for indigent patients for more than a decade. More than 600 specialists, 90 percent of them society members, participate, including about half the members of the Alachua County Dental Society. Over the past 10 years, $14 million in health care services have been donated to the sick and needy who have fallen between the health-care cracks. *Photo by Randy Batista/ Media Image*

Hospice of North Central Florida provides care and support to patients and their families facing terminal illness. In form and function, Gainesville's Hospice House (pictured here) does not resemble a hospital or nursing home, yet it provides a level of comfort and medical security to patients who do not require constant medical attention. *Photo by Ray Carson*

■ Roughly 29,000 people (not counting the University of Florida students, faculty, and staff who use the on-campus facilities) in Gainesville are members of one of six fitness centers in Gainesville. Each facility is challenged with the task of meeting the fitness needs of the town's diverse demographic: college students, stay-at-home moms, busy business people, senior citizens. Motives to join include losing weight, getting or staying in shape, and socializing with like-minded people. Age and condition seem to be no barrier to friendships formed on the treadmill. *Photos by Ray Carson.*

Gainesville's churches embody a myriad of faiths, communities, histories, and architectural styles. Historic Pleasant Street Church in the 5th Avenue district is a sentinel of the neighborhood's traditional glory as a teeming, vibrant African-American enclave. Friendship Baptist Church is another of the city's historical churches. *Photos by Ray Carson*

Gainesville may never have a white Christmas, but Christmas and Hanukkah lights brighten the holiday season throughout the city, casting a warm feeling throughout the its neighborhoods and businesses. Gainesville's Downtown Community Plaza hosts a New Year's celebration and a Christmas Festival of Lights. Horse-drawn carriages and music by local church and school groups herald the holiday season for young and old. Neighborhoods near downtown line their sidewalks with luminarias, softly lighting the way past colorfully decorated homes. *Photo by Ray Carson*

How does God look? Jesus? Angels? Since no one knows for certain, the artwork in churches performs a service in that it gives form to deities. The stained-glass windows in several Gainesville churches act as portals to the beyond, and are intricate works of art to boot. Some are true witnesses to saving grace and resurrection. The large "Ascension Window" at downtown's Holy Trinity Episcopal Church was sent out for repairs in 1991. It wasn't a few weeks later that the old, Gothic-style church with intricate wood carvings was burned to the ground - one of 30 Florida churches torched by an arsonist in 1991. It has since been reinstalled in the new sanctuary, along with French-made side windows. Molten pieces of the rest of the old windows have been refashioned into works of smaller art, which are quickly bought up by the many parishioners and loyal friends whenever they are offered at art festivals. *Photos by Ray Carson*

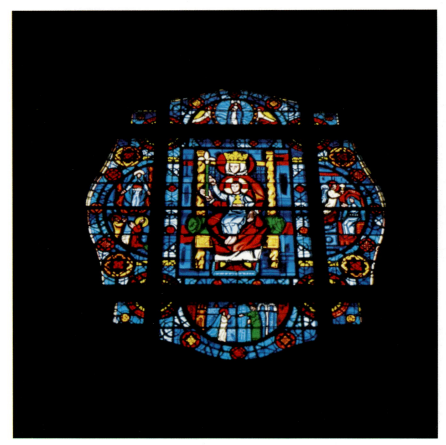

7

Chapter
Seven

Beauty of Life

Alligators: as much a part of Florida as swamps, pine woods, and sandy beaches. In fact, the native Alligator mississipiensis is found only in the Southeastern United States, from coastal Texas around Florida to the swamps of North Carolina. While they seem cute and helpless when they are born, they don't stay that way for long. They're not as large as they used to be: even a hundred years ago, gators measuring up to 18 feet were found in the Everglades. Adult males larger than 14 feet are rare today. Their fierce appearance is the result of not only 80 large, pointed teeth, but a major overbite, with bottom teeth neatly fitting into depressions when the mouth is shut. Alligators in captivity have broader heads—a possible indication of their more sedentary lifestyle. Their eyes are a silvery-taupe, but shine eerily green when a light hits them after dark, a method used by hunters on the annual alligator harvest allowed in various locations around the state. Gators' head-slapping and bellowing, as well as body posture, gives them a primeval demeanor. However, the beauty of gators is simply that they have been around so long. Alligators are remnants of a prehistoric era. When dinosaurs became extinct, these modern day contemporaries of dinosaurs continued to flourish. They live miraculously close to high-population centers, moving easily from natural pond to subdivision retention basin, and despite their penchant for live prey, there have been relatively few proven cases of unprovoked attacks and fatalities in the past 50 years. *Photo by Ray Carson*

◻ When the public display portions of Florida Museum of Natural History moved from cramped quarters on campus, out came the big guys: mammoths and other large prehistoric creatures that roamed eons ago now give people a glimpse of life as it was. Traveling and permanent exhibits run the gamut of Florida's natural history. *Photo by Randy Batista/ Media Image*

◻ Westside Park is a treed haven filled with playground equipment, tennis and basketball courts, adult softball and youth baseball fields, and a popular jogging/walking trail. A recreation center houses large bridge club gatherings and AARP meetings. Despite a Southern pine beetle infestation three years ago which felled dozens of mature Loblolly pines, it's still a popular spot. The only public pool on the west side of town is also on the grounds, an Olympic-size L-shaped pool featuring water slides for children and lap lanes for the fitness-oriented. *Photo by Ray Carson*

◻ (Opposite page) Rarely does a day go by that a traveler doesn't see a pack of bicyclists heading out to the many country roads surrounding the urban area. Bike paths are *de regieur*, and are heavily used. With nearly 50,000 college students in town, the bike is not just a form of recreation, it is a popular mode of transportation in town. As locals know, the wide open, seemingly endless space of Payne's Prairie makes it an ideal location for cycling and many other activities. Of all of Alachua County's natural features, Paynes Prairie is the most dominant. From the south, the 21,000-acre plain serves as a gateway for motorists along both U.S. 441 and Interstate 75. After more than a month of rain in early 1998, travelers were treated to a sight seen only three or four times in recorded history: the prairie became a full-fledged lake. *Opposite above by Randy Batista/Media Image, opposite below by Ray Carson*

■ Airboats, while reviled by many who cherish their peace and quiet, are revered by others who utilize the craft to reach areas too shallow for conventional craft. The drought in North Central Florida has rendered many areas formerly considered fishermen's meccas into swamps and drying sloughs. Orange Lake, once a 12,700-acre lake and one of Florida's top bass and bream fishing spots, is now a several-hundred-acre shallow pond dotted by grassy islands that are now taking root. The boat ramps have all closed. *Photos by Ray Carson*

A fisherman guides his bass boat along one of the numerous freshwater lakes and ponds in North Central Florida. There are uncounted navigable lakes in the area, thanks to the relatively shallow water table, and many of them are accessible to the public. *Photos by Ray Carson*

The Devil's Millhopper is the state's deepest dry sinkhole. It plummets 117 feet deep from the forest floor. The surrounding 63 acres have been designated a state park, and features a diorama on how sinkholes form, a guide to what kinds of flora and fauna will be found, and peaceful trails. The plant life along the walls and bottom of the sink are remarkably similar to species found in the North Carolina mountains. The temperature is almost always 20 degrees cooler than "up top." To those new to the area, it has become an unexpected respite from the outside world. Over the past decade, the formerly "out of the way" destination has found itself surrounded by high-price housing developments and a major shopping center. Despite this encroachment, the site has been carefully and lovingly protected.

For most of its life, The Devil's Millhopper was untamed. Students and local folk are full of stories of slipping and sliding down the steep walls to the bottom, where they could collect the abundant sharks' teeth. The sinkhole is nearly exactly between two coasts, and the sharks' teeth are testimony to Florida's past as an underwater ridge. However, years of such use—and occasional abuse—led to the building of a wooden walkway and stairway in 1976 that winds down to the coolness near the sink's floor. There are 232 steps down, with plenty of rest stops in between. As many can attest, it's easier and faster to get to the bottom than to return. *Photo by Ray Carson*

Phlox drummondi is one of the more prolific of North Florida's wildflowers. Vast patches of pink, lavender and occasionally white five-petaled flowers blanket country roadsides as well as interstate rights-of-way for several months in spring. The Florida Department of Transportation and garden clubs around the state have teamed up to sow more seeds in areas where color is lacking. DOT also cooperates by holding off roadside mowing until after flowering, thereby allowing the annuals to reseed and further naturalize. *Photo by Ray Carson*

(Opposite page) Florida is more than palm trees. Gainesville has been a Tree City USA since 1983. Tree City USA, sponsored by The National Arbor Day Foundation in cooperation with the USDA Forest Service and the National Association of State Foresters, provides direction, technical assistance, public attention, and national recognition for urban and community forestry programs. This home in the Historic Northeast District is across from the popular Duck Pond. *Photo by Ray Carson*

The 275-acre, city-owned Morningside Nature Center is home to a 10-acre living history farm, which features weekend tours to demonstrate how life in this area used to be. Different days are set aside to showcase spinning, gardening, animal husbandry, cooking, a 161-year-old cabin, some cows and sheep and pigs, a working wood-burning stove, and other items likely to be found on a farmstead established in the 1800s. *Photos by Ray Carson*

San Felasco State Park is 6,500 acres of wilderness. Hammocks, hardwood forest, sinkholes, streams, and a labyrinth of walking trails beckon hikers and horseback riders. the land was purchased in 1974 through the Florida Environmentally Endangered Lands Program, and has remained in pristine condition. Over the years, the park land has become surrounded by development; but stewards remain vigilant to protect it from any changes in resources. *Photos by Ray Carson*

■ Blue Springs is the epitome of a country swimming hole: Situated at the end of a long, dusty road and surrounded by tall trees, the spring is round, deep, crystal clear, and very cold—a fact that one is constantly reminded of as boys in baggy pants push squealing girls off the tall wooden platform into the 72-degree water. Picnic sites, a campground, and a boardwalk leading to the Santa Fe River, into which the spring runs, complete the scenario for simple summer pleasures. *Photos by Ray Carson*

Canoeing is a sport enjoyed by families as well as more advanced boaters. Along the more sedate Santa Fe River, even young and inexperienced paddlers can guide their craft along with the current. Adventure Outpost near High Springs offers canoe trips with pickup at Rum Island or Hollingsworth Bluff farther downriver; special night-time trips are offered during each full moon weekend. Canoeists can fully expect to see otters, Florida gar, a variety of birds, plentiful turtles, and even an occasional alligator along their trip. Beavers were once plentiful, and there are still signs of these rodents' chewing of trees along the bank. Much of the Santa Fe River, which acts as the northern border of Alachua County, is undeveloped. *Photos by Ray Carson*

Gainesville is a different Florida than what people may envision, and those who live here like it that way. There are seasons, distinct phrases in the year's sentence: winters that do require a heater, fireplace and coats; an exuberant and comfortable—albeit too brief—spring that segues into summer heat; a fall that features colorful leaves and a gradual chilling that fades back into winter again. Winters are dry; summers are wet; each season suits the plants that naturally grow here.

Photos by Ray Carson

▣ Gainesville Regional Utilities transformed a retention pond near its wastewater treatment facility into a set of nature trails and a park highly regarded by the local Audubon Society. The series of ponds serves as an alternative to deep-well injection, and helps filter more than a million gallons of treated wastewater a day. *Photo by Randy Batista/Media Image*

▣ (Below and opposite page) Kanapaha Botanical Gardens encompasses 62 acres and features specialty and display gardens: a vinery, carnivorous plants, palm, cactus, camellia, rose, perennial, wetland, and woodland. The gardens' lushness is attributable to the reclaimed water it uses, which is supplied by the neighboring GRU wastewater treatment facility. *Photos by Ray Carson*

Chapter Eight

Gainesville's Neighbors

Located southwest of Gainesville on the Gulf of Mexico, Cedar Key possesses a laid-back, old-Florida charm and some of the best fishing waters around. *Photo by Ray Carson*

■ Time stands still in some of the older communities in the Gainesville area, such as Micanopy. A mecca for antique collectors, Micanopy is in many parts an antique itself, a quiet place where the clock seems to tick a slower. The Herlong Mansion in Micanopy, an 1845 home that was renovated into a bed-and-breakfast about 15 years ago, features impeccably decorated period accommodations with names such as Pink's Room and the Governor's Suite. The ghost of Inez, the last full-time family resident and one of the daughters of the original owner, is said to haunt the hallways at night. Proprietor Sonny Howard relishes regaling guests with her bittersweet story, usually the morning after they have slept in her favorite room. More often than not, it explains the curious swishing of fabric and soft footsteps on the wooden floors reported by many overnight visitors. *Photos by Ray Carson*

If you can't get it at the Waldo Farmer's and Flea Market, you don't need it. Conversely, if you don't need it—especially if you don't need it—you probably will buy it there during a weekend visit. Peacocks, sweat socks, cheap earrings, fresh produce, real antiques, sailboat hardware, peaches, crocheted toilet-paper cover-ups in the shape of a Southern belle, Swiss army knives, and tractor tires—it's all there, and more. Lots more. The large market is open weekends on U.S. 301 just north of Waldo, a town in northeastern Alachua County. *Photos by Ray Carson*

■ No spot in Florida is more than 70 miles away from salt water. There is 1,350 miles of coastline, and, actually, 8,426 miles of shoreline if you count keys, islands, and permanent sandbars on the peninsula. A good portion of that is sandy beach, ranging from the fine, white powder of the Panhandle and West Coast to the gritty, pink sand of the upper East Coast. What isn't beach is mangrove, a plant that looks like it's growing on stilts; and houses around mangroves should likewise be on stilts, as the water is always high and the ground low in these spots.

When Gainesvilleans want to dip a toe into the Atlantic or just hike and picnic along the coastal trails, (pictured here) they head for Crescent Beach, just south of St. Augustine. This strip is jammed with high schoolers at spring break and families and college students during the summer. Other nearby beach retreats include Cumberland Island to the north; St. Augustine Beach and Anastasia Island; Ormond, Daytona, and New Smyrna; and, farther south, the surfing mecca of Cocoa Beach. While nearer strands exist along the Big Bend coastline, the narrow strips of dredged-up sand at Cedar Key, Dekle Beach, and Keaton Beach hardly qualify as beaches. *Photo by Ray Carson*

■ Located in historic downtown Orlando, Church Street Station offers some of central Florida's most unusual and exciting dining and shopping opportunities. *Photo by Ray Carson*

◻ Santa Fe Community College-Starke is housed in the historic Andrews Center, the former Bradford County Courthouse, built in 1902. Guy Andrews, a believer in higher education, initially pledged $200,000 to the renovation project, a pledge that eventually grew nearer to $1.5 million before the job was finished, including the purchase and paving of adjoining property for landscaped parking lot to accommodate 76 spaces. Other private donations totaled nearly $750,000. The satellite campus currently has an enrollment of about 500 students. *Photo by Ray Carson*

■ Home restoration has taken root in High Springs, with many older buildings showing efforts at renovation and a return to their original architectural style. High Springs was established on its present site in 1844. The current name was adopted in 1888, but the city wasn't incorporated until modern times. High Springs became an important railroad center in 1896 and phosphate mining, timber, and agriculture also added to the economy. But the city's growth and stability in the first half of the 20th century depended on the vitality of the steam-driven rail system. The railroad yard gradually closed down as diesel power replaced steam in the 1950s. The town's livelihood today depends largely on tourists who are drawn to its bed-and-break-fasts, antique shops, and the nearby springs and rivers. *Photos by Ray Carson*

O'Leno State Park is located north of High Springs and features a phenomenon rarely seen in nature: the Santa Fe River. Already 50 yards wide and flowing only somewhat lazily, the Santa Fe disappears suddenly underground and continues its path through a labyrinth of limestone caverns and fissures, re-emerging at River Rise Preserve State Park about three miles downstream. From there it continues its 40-mile course to join up with the fabled Suwannee River at Rock Bluff. Along the way, it is fed by numerous clear springs, some of them large in magnitude, such as Poe, Blue, and Ginnie, and some of which are smaller and feature local names like Rum Island and Devil's Eye. The pristine Ichetucknee—an icy river enjoyed by thousands of swimmers who float along for several miles on old inner tubes each day during the summer—feeds it about halfway to its final convergence. *Photo by Ray Carson*

Visitors to nearby St. Augustine can absorb the Spanish colonial charm and warm sunshine from the seats of a horse-drawn carriage.

◻ The Castillo de San Marcos, built between 1672-1695, served primarily as an outpost of the Spanish Empire, guarding St. Augustine, the first permanent European settlement in the continental United States. Although the Castillo has served a number of nations throughout its history (Spanish and British and then Spanish again), it has never been taken by military force. It is now a national park, consisting of original historic fortress and the surrounding 25 acres. It is the oldest European fortress built of stone blocks in the U.S. The blocks were made of coquina, cut in a quarry on nearby Anastasia Island. It was ideal material, because it was very porous and when cannonballs hit, the walls were not broken, but only dented. This porosity, however, allowed water to pass through the walls, which was bad not only for soldiers' health, but bad for food and really bad for gunpowder. To solve this problem, the outside of the fort was painted. The paint kept out much of the moisture; but being white, the paint also made the Castillo easier for ships to see. This water seepage has also created problems to the interior, and this portion of the fort is closed for a good portion of 2001 while repairs are made to the two gun decks, which were reinforced with concrete earlier this century. *Photo by Ray Carson*

◻ St. Augustine is the oldest city in the continental United States, so its many shops and stores cater to visitors who want a glimpse of the past. King Phillip II named Don Pedro Menendez de Aviles, Spain's most experienced admiral, governor of Florida. Menendez arrived off the coast of Florida on August 28, 1565, the Feast Day of St. Augustine. Eleven days later, he and a fleet of 11 ships, 500 soldiers, 200 sailors, and 100 others, landed at the mouth of the Matanzas River, naming the site San Augustin. *Photo by Ray Carson*

For most of America and, frankly, much of the world, Orlando, Florida, is synonymous with Walt Disney World, the mega-theme park that has changed the face of Central Florida. Most natives remember Orlando as a mid-sized burg dissected by I-4, and a pit stop on the way somewhere else. But Mickey and his entourage changed all that in the late 1970s when they purchased a swamp in the middle of nowhere and proceeded to turn it into more than 200 theme-park attractions. On their heels were Sea World, Universal Studios, and a plethora of spin-off restaurants, shopping districts, and hotel/motel complexes (there are more than 93,000 hotel rooms in the greater Orlando area).

But in the middle of this growth remain a few islands of constancy and peace. Lake Eola Park gives people a chance to paddle around a little lake, which takes up half of the 43-acre nature park in the middle of downtown, or jog its mile-long walking trail. A popular arts-and-crafts festival rings the lake in the spring and again in the fall, and a Shakespeare festival and Independence Day picnic in the park with fireworks draws families and visitors alike. Orlando is a good two-hour drive from Gainesville, a trek many people take to hook up with the International Airport there.

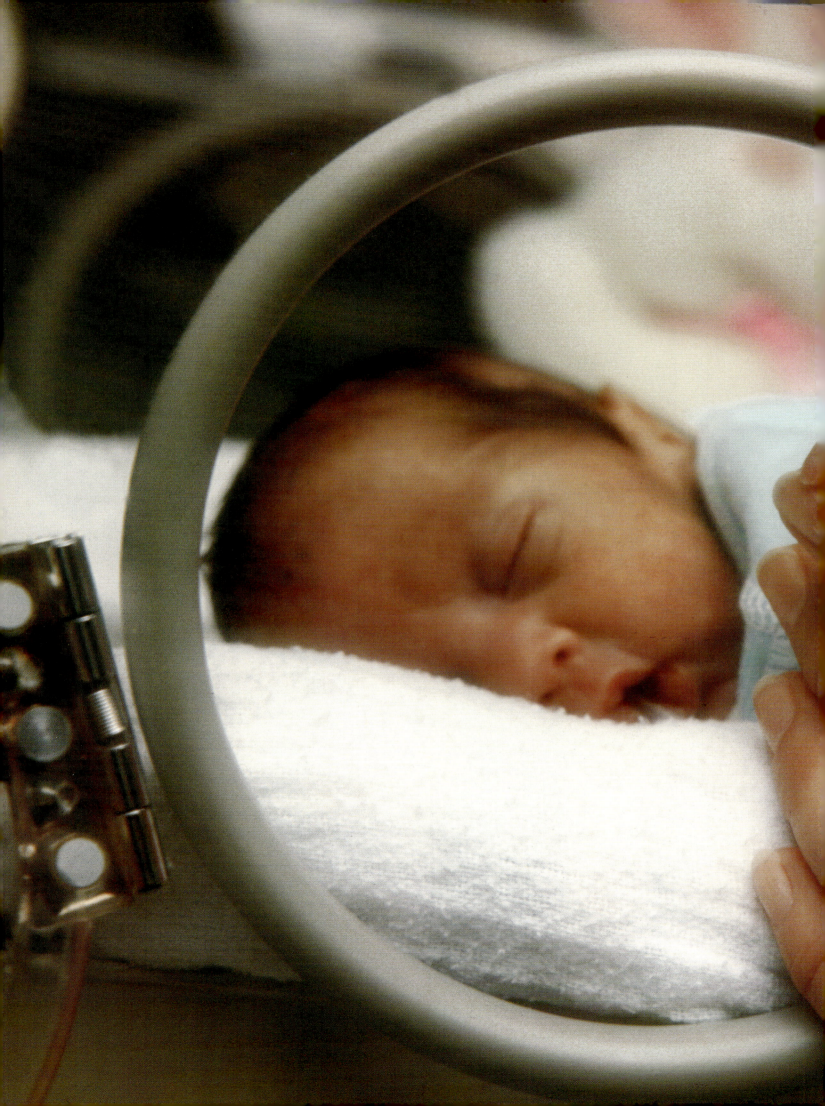

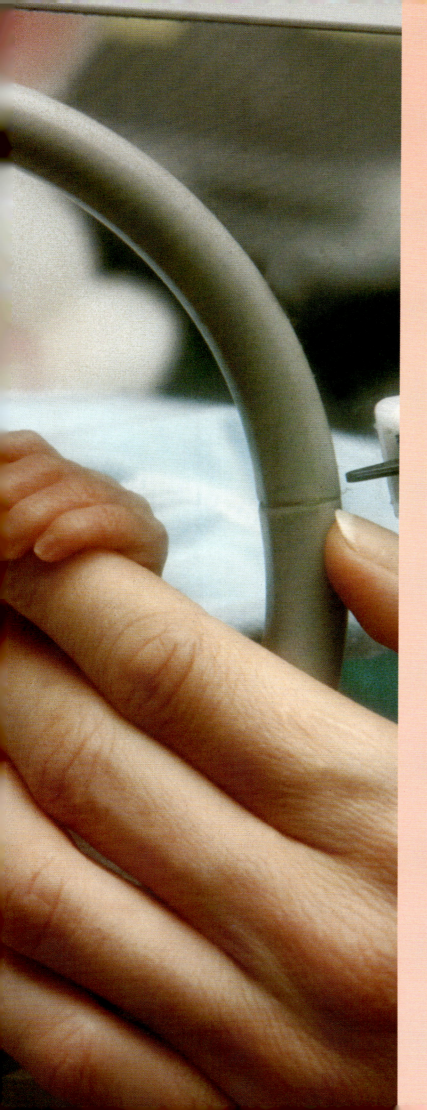

Chapter Nine

Health Care and Education, Quality of Life and Hospitality

From birth onward, residents of Gainesville enjoy access to some of the finest hospitals, schools, and civic institutions in the country.
Photo by Randy Batista/Media Image

SHANDS HEALTHCARE

As a not-for-profit health system affiliated with the University of Florida (UF), Shands HealthCare is founded on a mission to care for patients, advance medical knowledge, teach healthcare professionals, and help build healthier communities. Within the Shands system, service and science not only co-exist, but they are intrinsically connected.

The academic environment permeates Shands HealthCare. At its heart is the University of Florida Health Science Center, the focus for the education and research that drives the healthcare services provided throughout Shands. The Shands system in Gainesville includes Shands at the University of Florida, Shands Children's Hospital, Shands at AGH, and two unique specialty hospitals. The surrounding counties throughout northcentral Florida are home to three rural community hospitals, each part of the Shands family. In addition, Shands Jacksonville, an academic medical center located in northeast Florida, is affiliated with Shands HealthCare and the University of Florida.

Shands at the University of Florida

As the only teaching hospital in Florida that serves patients from every county, Shands at the University of Florida is specifically designed to care for those with the most complex health problems or chronic diseases. The hospital is recognized for its state-of-the-art facilities and technology, as well as the advanced level of care provided by the faculty of the UF Health Science Center and its College of Medicine.

Here patients can receive innovative treatments available at only a handful of medical centers in the nation. The transplantation program, for example, performs almost 450 organ and tissue transplantations each year and is ranked among the top programs in the country by the United Network for Organ Sharing (UNOS).

Such sophisticated programs require advanced clinical settings. In response to a growing demand for intensive care beds, the ICU facilities of Shands at UF are being expanded to offer additional

■ (Above) Shands Children's Hospital offers cutting-edge clinical programs while its healing environment addresses the medical, social, and emotional needs of young patients and their families.

■ (Below) Shands at the University of Florida is the only teaching hospital serving patients from every county in the state.

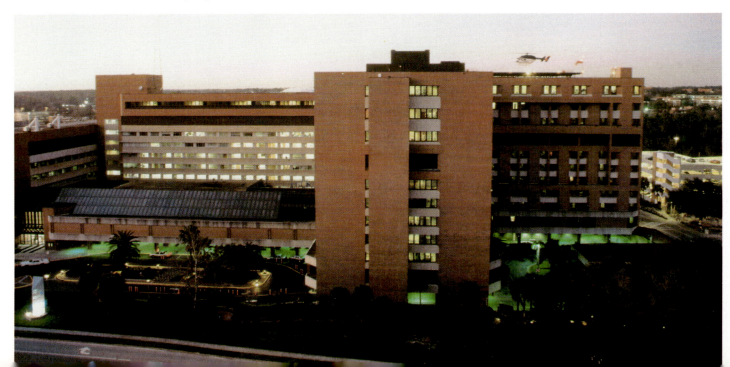

capacity for medical and surgical patients. At the same time, the pediatric programs and services will be reorganized to more clearly delineate Shands Children's Hospital.

Shands Children's Hospital

Shands Children's Hospital at the University of Florida is one of the largest pediatric facilities in Florida. This unique hospital-within-a-hospital provides treatment to infants and children through clinical programs and professional services built on the strength of the UF Department of Pediatrics.

It is home to one of only seven Children's Lung Centers in the nation, the largest pediatric transplant program in the state, and new epilepsy and sleep disorder services. UF pediatric surgeons are using a new approach for the treatment of diaphragmatic hernia, a life-threatening birth defect that impedes lung capacity and development and can also damage other internal organs. They have achieved survival outcomes that are approximately 30 percent higher than the national average survival rate for infants who receive traditional treatment for this condition. Other programs such as those offered in cell and organ transplantation, asthma, interventional cardiology and electrophysiology, diabetes, HIV, and critical care medicine put Shands Children's Hospital at the cutting edge of clinical treatment for children.

A top priority is creating an environment that addresses not only the medical needs of patients but also the social and emotional needs of these children and their families. Shands Children's Hospital sought out family members of patients to serve on the Family Advisory Committee and identify ways to make the hospital more family-friendly. The Family Resource Center, with its computer workstation, Internet access, and small library, is just one of this group's ideas that have been implemented as part of the hospital's commitment to sustaining a healing setting for seriously ill children and their families.

University of Florida Physicians

More than 750 faculty physicians practice at Shands hospitals and facilities throughout north Florida. These University of Florida Physicians are leaders in medicine today, combining pioneering research with unsurpassed clinical care.

Through the expansion of their specialty and primary care practices—including locations in underserved neighborhoods—these doctors have made healthcare accessible for area residents. And they are building stronger relationships with community physicians as part of their commitment to enhanced patient care.

The UF Shands Cancer Center is an interdisciplinary initiative that links UF physicians to offer patients the latest advances in diagnosis, treatment, and prevention of cancer. The center participates in numerous national clinical trials and protocols that bring the benefits of research to patients.

UF physicians are involved in a variety of multidisciplinary programs to attract patients throughout the region. The new Weight Management Program, developed in conjunction with the College of Medicine and Shands, provides long-term medical and surgical management of weight disorders. At the Executive Health Center, comprehensive medical evaluations, consultations, and treatment plans are offered in a private setting that includes a business center for patient convenience.

■ University of Florida physicians offer primary and specialty care services in Shands hospitals and facilities throughout the region.

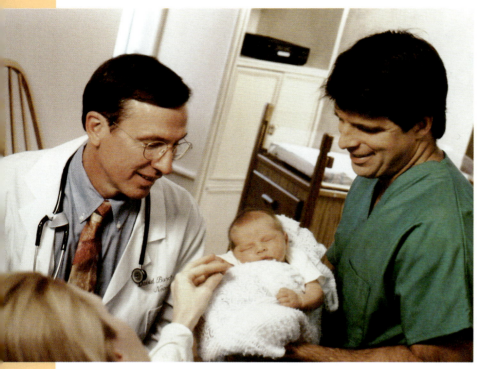

Shands Specialty Hospitals—Shands Rehab Hospital and Shands at Vista

Comprehensive care is the hallmark of Shands HealthCare. The specialty hospitals in the system make it possible to integrate specialized services into patient care, including physical rehabilitation and treatment for behavioral and psychiatric illnesses.

Shands Rehab Hospital is the only rehabilitation facility of its kind in the region, accredited by both the Joint Commission on Accreditation of Healthcare Organizations (JCAHO), the Commission on Accreditation of Rehabilitation Facilities (CARF), and the Florida Brain and Spinal Injury Program. It offers the most complete range of inpatient and outpatient rehabilitation services in the region, for patients ranging from spinal cord injury and stroke victims, to those recovering from amputations, burns, joint replacements, and transplant surgery.

Shands at Vista offers a community-based setting for treating patients with behavioral and psychiatric problems. The treatment team here collaborates closely with Shands at UF, the UF Department of Psychiatry, and private-practice and UF physicians. A comprehensive child and adolescent psychiatric inpatient program is also located at Shands at Vista. For the most complex patients, consultation services and diagnostic

■ Shands at AGH is a regional community hospital that emphasizes both patient focus and sophisticated care. The Shands at AGH healing philosophy encompasses body, mind, and spirit.

Shands at AGH

As a regional community hospital, Shands at AGH in Gainesville is distinct within Shands HealthCare, blending the patient focus of a community hospital with sophisticated services and programs made possible through collaboration with private-practice physicians, UF faculty, and Shands.

Shands at AGH is Florida's first community hospital to affiliate with Planetree, a nationwide alliance of healthcare facilities committed to creating a healing environment for body, mind and spirit. The Four East floor of the hospital has been renovated as part of the Planetree initiative with beautiful rooms and common areas that include a meditation space. Ongoing renovations of Shands at AGH include remodeling the lobby as well as patient floors for cardiology and obstetrics.

The make-up of the medical staff practicing on the Shands at AGH campus reflects the growing interrelationship between community physicians and UF faculty. UF urologists perform surgeries at Shands at AGH, and UF internal medicine physicians and neurosurgeons also have a presence on the Shands at AGH campus.

Shands at AGH cardiology services offer invasive and non-invasive interventional treatments and are being expanded with the development of a chest pain program in the ER and the addition of UF nuclear cardiology.

Collaborative programs such as these enable patients to obtain the most appropriate healthcare in the most convenient, efficient environment.

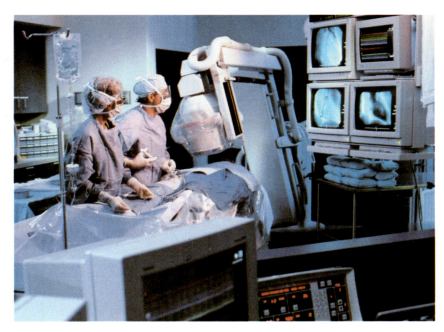

considered essential to the health of this medically underserved region. The additional funding and reimbursements it receives are being reinvested in programs and services to benefit the community, such as a new ambulatory care center, which houses a primary care practice and "fast track" emergency care program.

The rural hospitals of Shands HealthCare have a long tradition of community involvement and outreach, offering extensive education programs to promote good health among local citizens. With expanded services and resources, they are continuing to keep quality healthcare available, affordable, and convenient.

A Commitment to the Community

Shands HealthCare is the premier health system in the Southeast linked to one of the nation's top-rated academic health science centers, committed to delivering an unsurpassed level of care to people throughout Gainesville, and the surrounding communities. Its breadth of services is as diverse as those who come to its hospitals for care. The foundation of Shands' health system rests on its ability to deliver essential healthcare to those living within its local markets; to offer medical services that make Shands the preferred choice of people throughout the region; and to provide sophisticated treatments and highly-specialized care that draw patients nationwide. Through a dedication to this mission Shands is improving the health of people everywhere. ■

technologies are provided at Shands at UF, while Shands at Vista offers a community-based setting for those patients who have minimal medical complications.

The Florida Recovery Center at Shands at Vista offers services for diagnosing and treating individuals with chemical dependencies with both inpatient and partial-hospitalization programs.

One goal of Shands at Vista is to promote education about behavioral and mental health issues, working closely with area organizations, and through public service announcements and participation in screenings to reach residents throughout the region.

Shands Community Hospitals—Shands at Lake Shore, Shands at Starke, and Shands at Live Oak

Shands HealthCare's three community hospitals located outside Gainesville benefit from the medical expertise and state-of-the-art technology that comes from being part of one of the leading academic health systems in the nation. And so do the people they serve.

Located in Lake City with close proximity to I-10 and I-75, Shands at Lake Shore, serves a pivotal role as a healthcare provider for the region. In the fall of 2000, the Shands trauma network stationed a third helicopter in Lake City for improved response time in transferring trauma patients to the Level One Trauma Center at Shands Jacksonville or to other facilities in Gainesville or north Florida.

Shands at Starke is the main healthcare provider for residents of Bradford, Union, and parts of Clay Counties. As a state-designated rural hospital, it has received funding to make vital improvements in its facilities. In addition, a board-certified general and colorectal surgeon has joined the medical staff and the hospital has invested in new surgical and diagnostic equipment.

Residents of Suwannee County and the surrounding area count on Shands at Live Oak for care. Certified as a Critical Access Hospital, it is

■ The Shands HealthCare system includes two specialty hospitals—Shands Rehab Hospital, the only rehabilitation facility of its kind in the region, and Shands at Vista, a behavioral health hospital.

UNIVERSITY OF FLORIDA

The University of Florida (UF) is a public, land-grant research university. Today, it is one of the most comprehensive institutions of higher education in the United States, encompassing an impressive array of academic and professional disciplines. The oldest and largest of Florida's public universities, the University of Florida is a member of the prestigious Association of American Universities (AAU). Its faculty and staff are dedicated to the common pursuit of the university's threefold mission: education, research, and service.

■ The University of Florida's faculty and staff are dedicated to providing quality education from the undergraduate through the doctorate level, with an emphasis on research and scholarship. *Photo by Ray Carson*

Teaching students ranging from the undergraduate through the doctorate level is the fundamental purpose of the university. Research and scholarship are integral to the education process and to unlocking the secrets of the natural world. The term, "service," addresses the university's obligation to share the benefits of its knowledge in the public's interest. These three interlocking elements span all of the University of Florida's academic disciplines and multi-disciplinary centers. They represent the university's mission to lead and serve the needs of the nation, all of Florida's residents, as well as the public and private educational system of Florida.

On 2,000 acres within a 100,000-population urban area, the University of Florida operates out of more than 900 buildings, with more than 160 of them with classrooms and laboratories. UF's facilities have a book value of more than $800 million, with a replacement value of approximately $2.1 billion. The northeastern area of the campus is listed as a Historic District on the National Register of Historic Places. The 23 single-student residence areas house some 7,000 students, and five family housing villages are home to a married student population of 2,200.

The Florida Museum of Natural History is the largest natural history/anthropology museum in the Southeast, and among the top 10 in the nation. Its natural science collections contain more than 10 million specimens. The Samuel P. Harn Museum of Art, with more than 26,000 square feet of exhibit space, is one of the largest museums in the region. In 1999, the Harn Museum acquired an important work by the 19th century French Impressionist Claude Monet. Acquisition of the 1890 painting, titled *Champ d'avoine,* was made possible through a generous gift to the university. Recently, the Harn Museum received a $3.2 million gift, which is eligible for state matching funds, to construct a 20,000-square-foot sculpture atrium. The Center for Performing Arts attracts world-class symphony orchestras, Broadway plays, operas, and large-scale ballet productions to Gainesville. Each season of performances promises to be the best yet.

During 2000, the University of Florida opened the $1.58 million Baughman Center, a serene facility designed to provide an intimate setting for musical recitals, seminars, and meditative and contemplative uses. A $10.3 million two-phase renovation program is underway to expand and modernize Rhines Hall, providing 40,000 square feet of new labs and offices.

■ UF is proud to house some of the largest and most technologically advanced laboratories and research centers in the world. *Photo by Ray Carson*

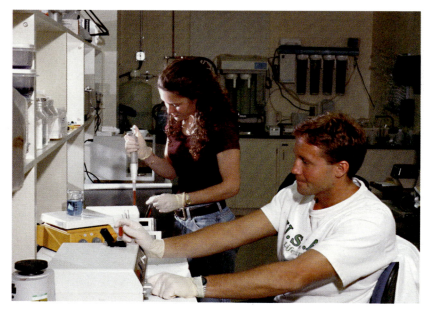

Other notable facilities include the world's largest citrus research center, the University Art Gallery, a laboratory capable of producing near zero degrees Kelvin—the coldest temperature in the universe, a world-class brain institute, an engineering research center for particle science and technology, a 100-kilowatt training and research reactor, the second largest academic computing center in the South, one of the nation's few self-contained intensive-care hyperbaric chambers, a public television and radio station, and two commercial radio stations. The university's Institute of Food and Agricultural Sciences (IFAS) is an extensive operation with facilities throughout Florida. As the 1990s closed out, a $12.1 million project consolidated three IFAS facilities into a new building in Apopka, north of Orlando. The building consists of 40,000 square feet of labs and offices, 11,000 square feet of teaching spaces, and 115,000 square feet of greenhouse and other environmental space. Nearly $3 million was spent to totally renovate the university's Aquatic Food Products Pilot Plant Facility.

As Florida's land-grant university, UF has a distinguished record of developing Florida agriculture into a national leader through research and extension services.

The university libraries consist of the main research library and six branch libraries throughout campus, along with the Health Science Center Library and the Legal Information Center. They form the largest information resource system in the state, containing more than 3 million volumes within its 10 million document holdings. Library collections are accessed through the computerized LUIS online system.

One of only 17 public land-grant universities in the esteemed higher education organization, the AAU, the University of Florida offers more programs on a single campus than all but a few U.S. universities. The University of Florida is a doctoral/research extensive institution as categorized by the Carnegie Foundation. It has 23 colleges and schools and more than 100 research, service, and education centers, bureaus, and institutes. More than 100 undergraduate majors are offered. More than 1,900 freshmen and sophomores participate in the honors program, which offers 90 to 100 honors courses per semester. The graduate school coordinates almost 200 graduate programs.

■ The university libraries form the largest information resource system in the state, containing more than 3 million volumes within its 10 million document holdings. *Photo by Ray Carson*

Professional degree programs include those offered in dentistry, law, medicine, pharmacy, and veterinary medicine.

Enrollment for fall semester 1999 totaled 44,276 students, including 36,049 in-state students representing all Florida counties with approximately 2,000 international students representing over 100 countries, with the remainder representing all 49 of the other states, the District of Columbia, Puerto Rico, and the Virgin Islands. The ratio of women to men during fall 2000 was 51 to 49. Other year 2000 statistics

■ Students enjoy a leisurely stroll between classes through the university's beautifully landscaped grounds. *Photo by Ray Carson*

■ The Ben Hill Griffin Stadium, or "the Swamp," is home to the University of Florida Gator Football Team as well as Gator Growl, the largest pep rally in the world. The university supports each varsity sport it fields and provides exciting athletic competition for fans and students alike. *Photo by Ray Carson*

in another nation. Faculty awards include a total of five faculty members receiving the Presidential Early Career Award for Scientists and Engineers since 1996. Also, in a national ranking of total Fulbright awards as of 1999, the University of Florida stands ninth among all public universities, with 15 of these arts and humanities awards.

The University of Florida has been awarded national scientific centers to include the McKnight Brain Institute for the study of neurological disease; the Engineering Research Center for Particle Science; and the National High Magnetic Field Laboratory in Tallahassee under the auspices of the University of Florida, Florida State University, and Los Alamos National Laboratory.

show that 75 percent of enrolled UF students are undergraduates, 18 percent are graduate students, and 7 percent are in professional degree programs. Approximately 22 percent of the UF student body members are minorities with 6.5 percent of the student population consisting of African-American students, 9.4 percent Hispanic/Latino students, and 6 percent Asian-American or Pacific Islander students.

University of Florida students are among the best in the nation. In 2000, approximately 90 percent of all entering freshmen scored above the national average on standardized college entrance exams taken by college-bound students. UF ranks fifth in the nation among public universities and seventh among all universities in the number of freshmen National Merit Scholars in attendance. Florida also ranks second among all public universities and fifth among all institutions in the number of National Achievement Scholars in attendance. Further, UF's freshmen retention rate of 91 percent speaks to the outstanding quality of the university's entire academic experience, from counseling to online programs to aid self-tracking of academic progress and class registration.

Aiding student development, UF has invested more than $7 million in campus computing infrastructure and $9 million in classroom renovations and technology upgrades in the last three years to meet the needs of modern education in an age of rapidly changing technology.

In addition to being academically motivated, students lead a rich social and extracurricular life. They belong to more than 450 student organizations on campus, attend more than 2,000 campus concerts, art exhibits and theatrical productions, guest lectures, sports contests, and other events a year.

A distinguished faculty of more than 4,000 attracted $339.4 million in research and training grants in 1999-2000. The University of Florida now has 54 Eminent Scholar Chairs. More than two-dozen faculty members have been selected to the National Academies of Science and/or Engineering, the Institute of Medicine, or a counterpart

The University of Florida basked in the glow of significant success with its varsity sports program during the 1990s. The UF Gators' thrilling run through the 2000 NCAA men's basketball tournament to the championship game indicates continued success into the new millennium. The university has made a strong commitment to support each varsity sport it fields and to provide exciting athletic competition for fans and student-athletes alike. In 1999-2000, for the ninth consecutive year,

■ A statue of former university president Marshall Criser sits beside Smathers Library East, the oldest library on campus, housing several outstanding collections including the Latin American collection, of which the university is extremely proud. *Photo by Ray Carson*

the University of Florida earned the SEC All Sports trophy, currently awarded by The New York Times Regional Newspaper Group, and presented to the student-athlete program that has achieved overall conference excellence in both men's and women's sports. Providing such effective management of the university's sports program is the University Athletic Association, a direct support organization serving as one of several component units of the university.

Aside from varsity sports, University of Florida students, faculty, and staff enjoy first-class recreational facilities. The Stephen C. O'Connell Center and the J. Wayne Reitz Union provide space for a myriad of activities. A thousand people can participate simultaneously in eight different recreational activities in the O'Connell Center, which seats 12,000 for concerts and other events. The O'Connell Center also is home to the Gator basketball, volleyball, swimming, and gymnastics teams. More than 25,000 use the Reitz Union daily for dining, meeting, bowling, pool and other table games, arts and crafts, music listening, television viewing, hotel accommodations, and more. The Student Recreation and Fitness Center was the first facility dedicated to recreation at the university when it opened in 1991, and now offers more than 100 fitness classes per week. The Southwest Recreational Center is a 64,000-square-foot facility located on the corner of a 26-acre site that features lighted outdoor basketball courts, tennis courts,

■ Century Tower is a campus icon built to commemorate the 100th anniversary of the university. Nestled beside it is the circa 1920s University Auditorium, one of several campus buildings included in the National Register of Historic Places and housing the Anderson Memorial Organ. *Photo by Ray Carson*

■ University of Florida students are academically among the best in the nation, but beyond their studies they lead a rich social and extracurricular life. The university not only provides numerous activities and organizations but also comfortable settings for students to fellowship and have fun, from the serene Baughman Center to several recreation centers to the great outdoors. *Photo by Ray Carson*

and a tournament-grade four-field softball complex. Additions to the recreation complex included $1.48 million for recreational fields and support building space. The university also offers a wide variety of intramural sports and hosts 40 sports clubs, from Aikido to water skiing and wheelchair basketball.

The University of Florida has earned a national reputation for being an excellent value. UF ranked 10th in *Money* magazine's 1998 College Guide, which described UF's program as among "the elite values in college education today." *Kiplinger's Personal Finance* magazine in September 1998 ranked UF fifth in its "Top 100 Values in State Universities." *U.S. News and World Report* in September 2000 rated UF 18th among all public universities. "Critical Comparisons," a college assessment service performed by educational professionals gave the University of Florida its "Good Work" Award in 1997. Given to those schools "that are holding the line against spiraling tuition costs while still managing to provide very competitive levels of service, resources, and safety," this award was presented to just six top research institutions out of the 64 examined. ■

Santa Fe Community College

*W*hen *Santa Fe Community College (SFCC) opened in 1966, fewer than 1,000 students were enrolled in classes. Today, 12,700 students take credit classes and more than 20,000 are enrolled in non-credit classes.*

"We have always been a student-centered college," said Dr. Larry W. Tyree, SFCC's president. "Our mission is to provide educational opportunity, responsiveness to the community, and innovation in the public interest."

Indeed the institution's impact has been far-reaching. SFCC serves students in Alachua and Bradford counties, and unlike most of Florida's community colleges, a large majority—two thirds—of its students enroll in the liberal arts. Many of these students transfer to the University of Florida. "Once they get to the University of Florida, our students earn, on average, the same grades and graduate in the same amount of time as students who start there as freshmen," said Dr. Tyree.

Serving students with numerous convenient locations and schedules helps SFCC meet the needs of its growing student body.

The Northwest campus, opened in 1972, is located near I-75 on 175 acres in northwest Gainesville. In 1985, the Andrews Center

■ Santa Fe's Information Technology Education programs are among the most popular courses taken by students.

opened in the renovated Bradford County Courthouse in Starke and expanded in 1991 with the addition of the restored Jones-Rosenberg Building. Built with private funds raised through a community campaign, SFCC's Blount Downtown Center now serves more than 1,000 students each term. The Blount Center is located in the renovated Sixth Street railroad depot with an addition nearby in the former Gainesville Gas building.

About 21 percent of SFCC students are over the age of 30 and many of those hold full- or part-time jobs. Night and Saturday classes at the Blount Center provide convenient times for class attendance around busy work and family schedules. Additionally, more than 1,000 students take classes via the internet.

"We are particularly proud of the helpful learning environment we have created for students at SFCC," said Dr. Tyree. "Our students are

more apt to succeed because of our smaller class size and a network of counselors, advisors, and programs." Academic advisors counsel students on which classes to take. The student development offices help students select careers, and developmental programs offer tutoring and personal attention for students having difficulty with a subject or class. Counselors help students with job placement before they graduate. "We are totally committed to the success of our students and think it is important for us to guide them throughout their college career so they do not waste their time or money," said Dr. Tyree.

The college's educational offerings include the Associate of Arts, Associate of Science, Associate of Applied Science, and Community Education programs. The Associate of Arts programs includes mainly liberal arts courses. Many students in this program intend to transfer to a four-year college or university. SFCC sends more students to the University of Florida than any other institution, public or private, in and out of the state. Many other SFCC students use the Associate of Arts degree as a terminal liberal arts degree or take courses for personal or career advancement.

SFCC's Associate of Science (A.S.) degree and certificate program, called Technology and Applied Sciences, consists of approximately 50 vocational programs that prepare students for entry into a career. Many of these programs also prepare students for transfer to a university. More than 90 percent of them either enter a career or go on to further higher education. These programs include Business; Computers; Graphic Design Technology; Autos, Homes, and Buildings; Health; Emergency Medical Services; Law Enforcement; Child Development; and Zookeepers, Managers, and Curators.

More than 20,000 local residents participate in SFCC's Community Education programs each year. Taken for personal enrichment or to learn specialized skills in a short-course format, courses range from swing dance, wine-tasting, and landscaping to needlepoint, computer skills, and parenting.

■ Award winning landscaping of Santa Fe's grounds is in harmony with North Central Florida's unique environment.

SFCC's Kirkpatrick Center retrains law enforcement and corrections officers and offers five classes a year to educate recruited officers. The center also has classes for state and federal officers.

The college's Center for Business and Professional Development serves as a liaison with the local business community. Working with a business, the college develops and custom designs courses to meet specific industry needs and offers classes at a SFCC campus or at the business location.

Campus life at SFCC also includes student clubs and activities along with intercollegiate and intramural athletics. Men's and women's basketball, fast-pitch softball for women, and baseball for men make up the college's intercollegiate programs.

Cultural activities enrich the lives of SFCC students and residents of the community. The Santa Fe Gallery, located at the Northwest Campus, features local and contemporary artists. Concerts, plays, and dance performances are offered regularly. The Dance Theatre of Santa Fe performs twice a year at UF's Phillips Center for the Performing Arts. SFCC's annual Spring Arts Festival draws 100,000 visitors to Gainesville and is one of the community's largest economic events. Another significant arts and economic event is Santa Fe's Starke Fall Festival, held annually in Bradford County.

Other SFCC attractions include its teaching zoo, which attracts 25,000 visitors annually, and a Florida cavern near Newberry, opening in 2001 as an educational facility for the public. The cavern, along with the Blount and Andrews centers and the Spring Arts and Starke Arts festivals, are developed through fundraising drives headed by Santa Fe's Endowment Corporation. The Endowment Corporation is a major source for private fundraising and community involvement and has been named one of the nation's best development offices for private fundraising. ■

RESIDENCE INN BY MARRIOTT

On a tree-filled site, just three miles from the University of Florida and two miles from downtown Gainesville, the Residence Inn by Marriott is one of Gainesville's most popular hotels. "Many of our guests are regulars who are like family to us," says General Manager Becky Hunt, who has been with the hotel since it opened in 1986.

The hotel includes 80 suites: 60 studio or one-bedroom suites and 20 penthouse suites, with two bathrooms, a bedroom, and a loft bedroom. All suites have fireplaces and full kitchens, with everything from cork screws and measuring cups to microwaves, full-size refrigerators, and dishwashers. The staff at the Residence Inn provides laundry pick up with same-day return, or guests can help themselves to the inn's on-site laundry facilities. No time to shop? No problem. Guests can leave their grocery list at the front desk in the morning and their groceries will be neatly put away in their suite, their account charged for the cost of the groceries.

Mornings start with complimentary breakfast, served in the hotel lobby. Guests can take their pick from a vast selection that includes scrambled eggs, Belgian waffles, oatmeal, bagels, muffins, dry cereal, fresh fruit juice, yogurt, coffee, and tea. *The Gainesville Sun* and *USA Today* are always available during breakfast hours. Monday through Thursday afternoons and University of Florida football game Fridays, hospitality hour is featured in the lobby. Beer, wine, sodas, and light snacks are available.

Amenities at the Residence Inn are impressive. There's a swimming pool and jacuzzi, gas grill and picnic tables, volleyball and basketball courts, and an exercise room with treadmill, stationery bike, and three-station universal machine. Add to those special extras: a toy box for children and a library with books, games, and cards for guest checkout. All suites have TV with cable and HBO and desks equipped with data ports. A "first-nighter" kit is provided in every suite with coffee, popcorn, tea, sugar, salt, and pepper.

The Residence Inn team is happy to help guests find the perfect restaurant or direct them to local businesses, shopping, performing arts and theater excursions, or other local attractions.

Guests in need of a hotel that will take pets, should look no further. "We've had everything here from pot-belly pigs to snakes and birds," says Hunt. A deposit is required for all pets, but they are welcomed in the inn.

"Women especially like the Inn," says Hunt, "because of our homey atmosphere, separate entrances, and no hallways."

Special rates for hospital patients, corporate, and government are available. ■

CABOT LODGE

One of Gainesville's most popular business hotels, Cabot Lodge welcomes its guests with warmth, comfort, and top-notch service. An attractive lodge-like atmosphere and atrium greet guests as they enter the lobby. A rustic décor of dark green hues complementing natural wood and a stone fireplace makes for a comfortable, homelike atmosphere. Located at I-75 and Archer Road, Cabot Lodge is just minutes from the University of Florida, Shands Medical Center, and Veterans Administration Hospital.

All 208 guest rooms offer amenities including satellite television, movie channels, and direct-dial telephones with data ports and free local calls. Three different types of elegantly appointed rooms are available: those with two double beds, one king bed, and the spacious executive king room that includes a private balcony, larger television, bathrobe, added toiletries, and a coffee maker. Children under 17 stay at no charge. Complimentary replacement toiletries and travel necessities are available with a quick call to the front desk.

An outdoor swimming pool, lending library, and exercise room are available to all guests. The Lodge Post is a 24-hour business center that provides free copies, fax service, and computer with printer and Internet access.

The Cabot Lodge is one of the area's first hotels to feature complimentary breakfast and cocktails, and it has become famous for its deluxe continental breakfast which includes oatmeal, fresh fruit, pastries, bagels, assorted breads, croissants, juices, coffee, milk, and of course—the morning newspaper. The two-hour evening cocktail reception features a full bar, homemade popcorn, and the opportunity to unwind and meet with fellow guests.

Manager Bart Johnson has been with Cabot Lodge for eight years and manages a team of 50-plus employees, the majority of whom are

■ Lodge-like atmosphere and atrium greet guests as they enter the lobby.

long-term employees. "We truly have the most capable staff in Gainesville. We can help with special requests at any time," he says. "We are constantly improving the Lodge. Instead of undertaking massive renovations, we upgrade and replace as needed, so the hotel is fresh and brand new for every guest."

Small meetings are a specialty of Cabot Lodge. Recently upgraded, the boardroom holds up to 14 guests. The larger meeting room holds up to 40, with various seating arrangements to accommodate each group.

Although the hotel stays busy, be sure to book ahead if you are coming during peak times—mid-January through April. Repeat customers make up 80 percent of the Lodge's business; while 70 percent of guests are business travelers.

An active community participant, Cabot Lodge is a member of the Gainesville Area Chamber of Commerce, the Gainesville Sports Organizing Committee, the Alachua County Hotel Association, and the Scholarship Club at the University of Florida.

"Our goal is to provide customers with a quality stay that is both safe and enjoyable. We cater to their needs," says Johnson. "Once we get people in the door, they see that we are the best value for a quality stay."

Cabot Lodge is owned and managed by Mississippi Management Inc., one of the nation's most highly respected hotel management companies. ■

■ Located at I-75 and Archer Road, Cabot Lodge is just minutes from the University of Florida, Shands Medical Center, and Veterans Administration Hospital.

AvMed Health Plan

As *Florida's only statewide not-for-profit HMO, AvMed Health Plan is dedicated to providing its members with the highest quality health care.*

■ With a strong focus on wellness and preventive care, AvMed offers a variety of workplace screenings and clinics. *Photo by Pierre Blanchet*

AvMed is one of only three HMOs in the nation to hold full accreditation from the National Commission on Quality Assurance and the Joint Commission on Accreditation of Healthcare Organizations. "We're proud to be accredited by our country's two top quality monitoring organizations," said AvMed President and Chief Executive Officer Robert C. Hudson. "It shows that we've been recognized for complying with rigorous national performance standards that promote quality health care."

AvMed also makes top grades in member satisfaction as the only statewide HMO to earn a five-star rating for member satisfaction by the Florida Agency for Health Care Administration.

That member satisfaction is the focus of AvMed's commitment to achieving its mission: "to improve the health of our members and communities by making health care more accessible and affordable while operating within the not for-profit humanitarian tradition."

Headquartered in Gainesville and Miami, AvMed has deep roots in North Central Florida, having merged in 1986 with SantaFe HealthCare, at that time a Gainesville-based hospital company.

In 1996 the company turned its full attention to health maintenance and illness prevention. An agreement with Shands turned operation of the hospitals over to them. Today, AvMed encourages its members to have routine physician visits and physicals, well-baby examinations, well-woman examinations, immunizations, and the earliest possible detection of disease processes.

Special programs for AvMed members include a toll-free 24-hour-a-day telephone line staffed by registered nurses for questions and health information. Non-medical questions can also be answered through toll-free phone calls to Member Services representatives, 24 hours a day. Mobile wellness programs give employers an opportunity to offer workplace screenings for breast cancer, skin cancer, bone density, prostate cancer, cholesterol tests, and flu shot clinics, even for employees who are not AvMed members. AvMed members who reach weight loss goals through Weight Watchers are reimbursed for fees paid, and members who want to quit smoking can receive discounted Smokenders Kits. Through AvMed's Care Management Programs, individuals at risk for congestive heart failure, asthma, and high-risk pregnancies are assigned personal nurses who teach them how to manage their conditions.

As a not-for-profit health plan, AvMed has no financial obligation to shareholders. "Because we're not-for-profit, we're able to better focus on our central mission of improving people's health and well-being," said Hudson. "Our profits go back into new or expanded services for our members and communities."

Providing primary and preventive health care and education, raising funds for worthwhile causes, and assisting in meeting the health care needs of the underserved are some of the ways AvMed puts its earnings back into communities.

In Gainesville, AvMed employs more than 400 and puts more than $13 million into the county's economy through its annual payroll. In 1999, AvMed was named Corporate Citizen of the Year by the Gainesville Council for Economic Outreach. ■

■ AvMed actively encourages members to take advantage of routine physicals, well-woman exams, and well-baby exams. *Photo by Bill Wax*

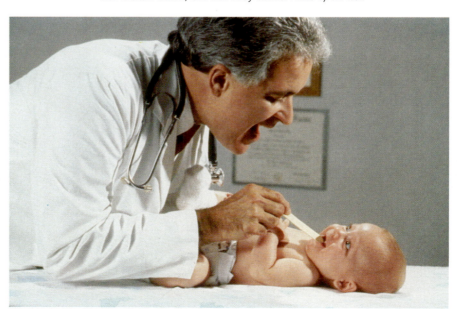

Chapter
Ten

Communications and Energy, Manufacturing and Distribution

Communications and energy networks are the lifeblood of modern industry. Thanks to Gainesville's strength and efficiency, several large manufacturers and distributors have made their home in or near the city. *Photo by Randy Batista/Media Image*

GAINESVILLE REGIONAL UTILITIES

Gainesville Regional Utilities, or GRU, is Gainesville, Florida's community-owned utility provider. GRU serves approximately 80,000 customers in metropolitan Gainesville with quality products and services, including electricity, natural gas, water, wastewater, and telecommunications.

■ GRU's downtown Administration Building offers handy "one-stop shopping" for electric, natural gas, water, wastewater, and telecommunications services. Its customers enjoy convenient combined billing with several payment options.

workshops, books, and videos on energy topics; and infrared scanning to identify abnormal heat and prevent maintenance and safety problems.

GRU has also been designated an Energy Star Building ally by the U.S. Environmental Protection Agency and the U.S. Department of Energy. In this capacity, GRU helps recognize commercial buildings with superior energy performance. Local builders also can earn the Energy Star Label for homes they construct, letting consumers know the structure has met strict requirements for energy conservation and performance.

In addition to the key role GRU plays in business activities of the community, GRU employees contribute hundreds of hours to worthy volunteer and civic-oriented programs in the area. GRU recently earned the National Community Service Award from the American Public Power Association.

GRU's reclaimed water program is an environmentally responsible concept that both reduces the demand on the community's drinking

As one of the area's largest businesses, GRU employs more than 750 people. Owned by the people of Gainesville, GRU is a good corporate citizen, recognized as the 2000 Business Leader of the Year by the Gainesville Area Chamber of Commerce. Each year GRU makes a financial transfer to the City of Gainesville that helps fund essential governmental operations such as police and fire protection, recreation, parks, and transportation.

In addition, GRU is actively involved in the business community, working with hundreds of small and large businesses to provide economic services through its "Business Partners Program."

"We partner with businesses so they can take advantage of our expertise in energy management and conservation," says Steve Stagliano, senior account representative. In return, local businesses agree to select GRU as their exclusive energy provider and receive discounted utility rates.

GRU provides a number of services to its business partners, including commercial audits by conservation specialists; evaluation of commercial and rental lighting systems to identify energy saving options; power quality monitoring to determine possible equipment problems;

■ GRU's "Electrifying Celebration" draws thousands each year to watch entertainment such as these jugglers as well as live bands, clowns, University of Florida Cheerleaders and Dazzlers, GRU bucket truck rides, and much more. GRU also provides informational booths to celebrate its commitment to the community.

water supply and reduces the quantity of wastewater that must be disposed of by other means. Wastewater treated to irrigation standards supplies free water to three GRU constructed water gardens, soccer fields, golf courses, the Veteran's Memorial, and some area neighborhoods. GRU's largest reclaimed water project is a beautiful nature park, including Chapman's Pond, which supports community recreation and wildlife habitat.

Taking care of the environment is an important part of GRU's corporate philosophy. "We strive to combine smart business practices with environmentally compatible, community-friendly solutions," says Mike Kurtz, GRU's general manager.

In order to meet Gainesville's growing power needs, GRU built an environmentally sound combined-cycle natural gas-fired 110-megawatt electric generating unit at the downtown J. R. Kelly Generating Station. Community consensus for the project was achieved by involving neighbors and citizens in the design process. As part of the overall project, GRU worked with other local agencies to help revitalize the surrounding neighborhood. This new generating unit not only helps reduce generation costs, but it also provides for improved air emissions and fuel efficiency.

Another important environmental concern at GRU is providing reliable electric service while protecting Gainesville's beautiful tree canopy. "We have reduced the number of distribution-related outages significantly because of our proactive and effective approach to vegetation management," said Dave Beaulieu, GRU's assistant general manager for Energy Delivery. GRU replaces problem trees through an annual tree giveaway and a successful trade-a-tree program.

■ GRU offers free public tours of its plants and facilities for students and organizations in the community. This group of students is taking a tour of the Deerhaven Generating Station, learning how GRU turns raw fuel sources such as environmentally friendly natural gas and low-sulfur coal into electricity.

■ GRU has recently constructed "Chapmans Pond Nature Trails," a public park with ponds, streams, waterfalls, and general irrigation provided through reclaimed water. The park attracts an abundance of wildlife, such as these beautiful birds, and serves as a conservation demonstration for the attractiveness and safety of reclaimed water.

Community aesthetics also are an important part of electric planning, which is why GRU is among the leaders in undergrounding electric facilities in the state of Florida. An aggressive program of installing protective aerial cable in neighborhoods throughout the community continues to improve GRU's already excellent record of reliability.

GRU's water and wastewater systems are among the best. The Murphree Water Treatment Plant has been recognized for excellent operations numerous times. The Kanapaha Water Reclamation Facility is one of only two plants in Florida permitted to discharge drinking water quality effluent directly into the aquifer.

GRU's natural gas system provides a safe, affordable, environmentally friendly energy alternative, making natural gas the natural choice for many GRU customers.

The newest GRU service is GRUCom, a communications utility offering high-speed, high-capacity data-transmission services. Also available are high-bandwidth services for commercial customers. For residential customers, GRU.Net's dial-up and high-speed Internet service provides fast, dependable fiber optic-supported service at among the lowest rates available in the area.

GRU and its employees are proud to be actively concerned members of the Gainesville community. From the best possible utility rates, products, and services, to the convenience of combined billing, to the concern of employees who also are neighbors, GRU exists to serve the needs of Gainesville. ■

GILLEN BROADCASTING

*I*n *a world where mega-corporations are the norm, KISS 105.3 is the exception. WYKS President and General Manager Doug Gillen has made Gainesville his home for the last 15 years and has helped focus the radio station on serving in a multitude of ways.*

"We really felt KISS 105.3 had to reflect the look and feel of Gainesville," said Gillen, "in both the on-air product and live appearances."

So, the Gillen family, parents Al and Doris, along with brothers Jeff and Doug, set out to create "Gainesville's Gator Party Station!"

Al's experience as chairman of Knight Ridder Broadcasting proved essential in creating a corporate philosophy that focused on a commitment to the audience and clients through superior services and products.

"Listeners and clients are the foundation of our business. Our only true asset is our ability to serve them," Gillen said. "In all our dealings, we continue to be forthright and strive to serve their best interests."

And it has worked. KISS 105.3 went from a station with an 18-month ratings decline to a perennial powerhouse. KISS 105.3 is now a leader for adults 18-49 and 21-49 with household incomes of $50,000+.

The KISS 105.3 Giant Boom Box is a staple at all the major events in Gainesville. The Party Patrol is on the streets of the community an average of 20 to 30 times per month giving out free food, drinks, and prizes.

And the station is heavily involved in a number of community service activities. KISS 105.3 kicks off the yearly March of Dimes

■ Back row, from left: Erin Sims, Jeff Marsh, Todd Steele, Chris Singleton, Mike Forte. Front row, from left: Sean Davis, Charlie Sternberg, Doug Gillen, Ashley Gillen, Jeri Banta, Laura Banta, Bradley Fuller, Mark Page, David Russell, Carrie Pyle, Courtney Becker, Jessie Wagner, Jennifer Bates, Kevin Quinn, Dena Hart.

■ Radio Disney Promotions Director, Jennifer Bates.

■ Children enjoy games and activities at a Radio Disney AM 1390 event.

Walk America, hosts Project Graduation, and works with every major non-profit organization in the city.

But that doesn't interfere with having fun. "We've made 6,000 gallons of Jell-O to give away a car and had our own version of drag races during the Gator Nationals," said Jeri Banta, program director.

The commitment to Gainesville extends beyond on-air. KISS 105.3 regularly hosts students for career shadowing, conducts numerous tours for youth groups, and regularly hosts and feeds a community church group.

"We need to stay in touch," Gillen said. "We really, really care about our community, our listeners, and our advertisers. In today's world, we think it is vital to be in touch with our listeners and our clients. We have real people—no voice mail. You get a real person who can focus on the reason for your call."

Most part-time employees at Gillen Broadcasting are students at the University of Florida or Santa Fe Community College. KISS 105.3 offers an incredible opportunity for them to earn a paycheck while gathering invaluable real-world broadcasting experience. Many former KISS 105.3 announcers have gone on to lucrative careers in Atlanta, Orlando, Chicago, and other cities across the country.

While some radio program directors and business managers bounce from one company to another as stations are bought and sold, KISS 105.3's Jeri and Laura Banta chose to stay with Gillen Broadcasting.

The Bantas agreed with the philosophy of Gillen Broadcasting and wanted to raise their family in Gainesville, a city that was later awarded *Money* magazine's Number One City Award.

Jeri and Laura continue to be instrumental in the successful operation of Gillen Broadcasting. Both Jeri and Laura work with listeners,

■ KISS 105.3 Air Personalities, Mike Forte and Kevin Quinn.

community service organizations, and advertisers to provide the highest-quality community radio station possible.

Recently, Gillen Broadcasting was successful in negotiating an agreement to air Radio Disney in Gainesville. Radio Disney is the only way local advertisers can join Disney in marketing to children and families. Radio Disney AM 1390 is Gainesville's own Disney station that offers its listeners and advertisers a chance to experience the Disney magic.

"Kids are "wanted" by virtually every company in America...as customers for life. Today, marketers realize that children as young as two can influence everything from where the family will vacation to the next car in the garage. It seems the amount of money children spend or influence is far greater than many marketers previously believed." Radio Disney was created, in part, as an avenue for local businesses to create loyalty from children and families. Adds Debbie Solomon, senior researcher at J. Walter Thompson advertising agency, markets also know that kids form brand loyalties as early as age two. (Source: *USA Today* 12/19/99) ■

U.S. CELLULAR

U.S. *Cellular is the nation's eighth largest wireless telecommunications provider. Recognized as an industry leader, U.S. Cellular provides superior-quality wireless service in the Gainesville area and to more than three million customers in 25 states.*

problem by loaning wireless phones preprogrammed to emergency 911, so victims of abuse can call for help at any time.

U.S. Cellular associates are also actively involved in supporting local business, civic, and charitable community organizations, serving on boards such as the Gainesville Chamber of Commerce, United Way, and March of Dimes.

Based in Chicago, U.S. Cellular has provided service to Gainesville since 1982 and strives to make wireless communications simple, personal, and affordable. U.S. Cellular is listed and traded as USM on the American Stock Exchange. For more information about U.S. Cellular, visit the company's Web site at www.uscellular.com. ■

Locally, U.S. Cellular has four retail offices with staff trained to meet business and personal wireless communication needs. Wireless services offered include: digital, short messaging, Internet text messaging, and nationwide caller I.D. A new service, SpanAmerica, offers customers nationwide toll-free calling and no roaming charges within the Southeast.

Dedicated to the communities in which it serves, U.S. Cellular has expanded its national community relations programs through targeted efforts that touch the lives of many, including the homeless, school children, domestic violence victims, and people seeking safer neighborhoods. U.S. Cellular community relations programs in the Gainesville area include:

Opportunity Calls SM: U.S. Cellular works with homeless shelters and violence prevention programs to donate cellular voice mailboxes to homeless and underprivileged individuals.

Cellular S.T.A.R.S. SM **(Student Training and Rescue Sessions** SM**):** This is a program designed to teach local elementary school students how to dial emergency 911 on a wireless phone.

C.A.L.L. SM: U.S. Cellular donates wireless phones preprogrammed to emergency 911 to groups that can affect public safety.

S.A.F.E. SM **(Stop Abuse From Existing** SM**):** This program provides victims of domestic violence with the tools they need to stop the cycle of abuse. Victims can receive wireless phones preprogrammed to emergency 911.

H.O.P.E. SM **(Homeless Outreach Phone Effort** SM**):** Reconnecting homeless and underprivileged people with their friends and family on Thanksgiving, U.S. Cellular provides free calls to anywhere in the continental United States.

H.E.L.P. SM **(Hometown Emergency Loaner Phones** SM**):** U.S. Cellular provides emergency organizations with wireless phones and service during times of disaster.

S.A.F.E. for Seniors SM: U.S. Cellular is addressing the elder abuse

MOLTECH POWER SYSTEMS

At its Gainesville corporate headquarters, Moltech Power Systems designs and manufactures rechargeable batteries for businesses and consumers throughout the world. The company specializes in advanced nickel-metal hydride, nickel cadmium, and lithium cell technologies. It also designs innovative batteries for manufacturers of portable devices, such as power tools, housewares, computers, cellular phones, and other portable electronics.

Moltech Power Systems is a wholly owned subsidiary of Moltech Corporation of Tucson, Arizona, with operations throughout North America, Asia, and Europe. The company employs 500 in Gainesville and 1,500 globally.

"We are particularly proud of our ability to cater to the needs of our customers and the unique requirements and specifications of their products. We work closely with our customers from the design of a product through production to create the ideal battery solution," said Joe Fisher, president of Moltech Power Systems.

The Gainesville facility is the home of Moltech's cell manufacturing, testing, engineering, and research and development operations. This facility also serves as the headquarters for all marketing, business development, sales, and customer service functions of the company. Moltech's facility in Juarez, Mexico, is North America's largest battery assembly facility. In addition to assembly, the Juarez plant handles battery design, intelligent electronics design, integration, cell formation, and testing. Moltech's European headquarters is located in Newcastle-under-Lyme, United Kingdom. Here regional battery design and assembly needs are handled, along with sales, marketing, and technical support. Moltech's Asian headquarters is located in Hong Kong. This site provides battery design and assembly, intelligent in-pack electronics development, regional sales, marketing, and engineering support. Sales offices are located throughout the United States, Europe, and Asia.

With almost 40 years of experience in the rechargeable battery industry, Moltech is an expert in meeting the portable power needs of leading device manufacturers. Customers include Makita Corporation, Kyocera, Qualcomm, Milwaukee Electric Tools, Sunbeam, Hewlett Packard, and Energizer.

In 2000, Moltech introduced Millennium®, its line of consumer rechargeable batteries for digital cameras, portable audio players, camcorders, cellular phones, and other power-hungry electronics.

■ Moltech manufactures individual cells and battery packs with smart electronics.

Moltech Power Systems is an active participant in the community and a supporter of children and science education. The company provides numerous educational programs in local schools and sponsors an after-school tutoring program at the Boys and Girls Club of Alachua County. Other sponsorships include Alachua County Junior Achievement, March of Dimes, United Way, American Cancer Society, and youth sporting activities throughout the community. "We are proud to call Gainesville home," Fisher says. "We are grateful for the support we have received and will always do our best to support programs, events, and organizations that improve the lives of the people who live here." ■

■ Moltech Power Systems' Alachua, Florida, facility serves as the company's global headquarters.

TOWER COMMUNICATIONS, INC. _____

*T*he phones are ringing, your Web page is getting plenty of traffic, the orders are rolling in. Enter Tower Communications, Inc., the parent company of United Southern Telecom (UST).

UST is a full-service call center and distribution business, specializing in order taking, data management, and product shipment.

With more than 6,300 square feet and 30 agent stations, UST is among the largest call centers in the Southeast. UST operates an international call center that serves clients throughout the United States and Europe.

"Our call center operates 24 hours a day, seven days a week. We take and process orders over the telephone, Internet, e-mail, fax, and regular ground mail," said Timothy P. Becks, president.

UST also handles out-bound business-to-business calls, as well as ticket sales for events such as PGA tournaments and NHRA racing.

UST's customer service agents are carefully screened and trained. "Our access to an educated pool of labor from the University of Florida and Santa Fe Community College has been a big selling feature for us," Becks said.

Distribution/fulfillment involves storage and shipping of products as orders are received. The company maintains its own climate-controlled and security-monitored warehouse. From its strategic location, UST is able to reach 66 million people with second-day delivery.

"The direct marketing industry is changing rapidly. E-commerce, TV advertisers, and catalog merchants have come to realize, to compete with retail, they must get their products into their clients' hands quickly. Two days from the phone to the home or the mouse to the house, is our goal," Becks said.

■ Operating under the service names of United Southern Telecom (UST) and Answer-Rite *Nationwide*, Tower Communications, Inc., is one of the nation's leading inbound/outbound call center, warehousing, and order fulfillment companies.

■ Staffed 24 hours a day, 7 days a week, Tower Communications, Inc., offers professional multi-lingual business messaging, telesales, live Web agent, and interactive voice mail services.

For international shipments, UST is strategically located within easy access to three international airports: Jacksonville, Orlando, and Tampa. It is also close to two international shipping ports: Jacksonville and Tampa.

In a business that serves thousands of customers a day, reliability is important, and UST delivers. The company is fully insured and accredited by the American Telemessaging Accrediting Counsel (ATAC). In addition, all the firm's computer systems are fully redundant and supported by generator power to insure 24-7 dependability.

Answer-Rite Nationwide is Tower Communications, Inc.'s business messaging division. "We serve a select clientele who prefer a human response to their customer calls," said Becks. "These are quality organizations who understand customer service." All Answer-Rite Nationwide agents receive 40 hours of training, and the company digitally archives messages for three years.

"Our clients are comprised of large organizations with multi-facilities located around the state and across the country," said Becks. "These businesses require the dependability and reliability that only an accredited call center can provide."

In addition to recruiting international businesses to Alachua County and providing good, high-paying jobs with full benefits, Tower Communications, Inc., supports many local charitable, community, and sponsored events. ■

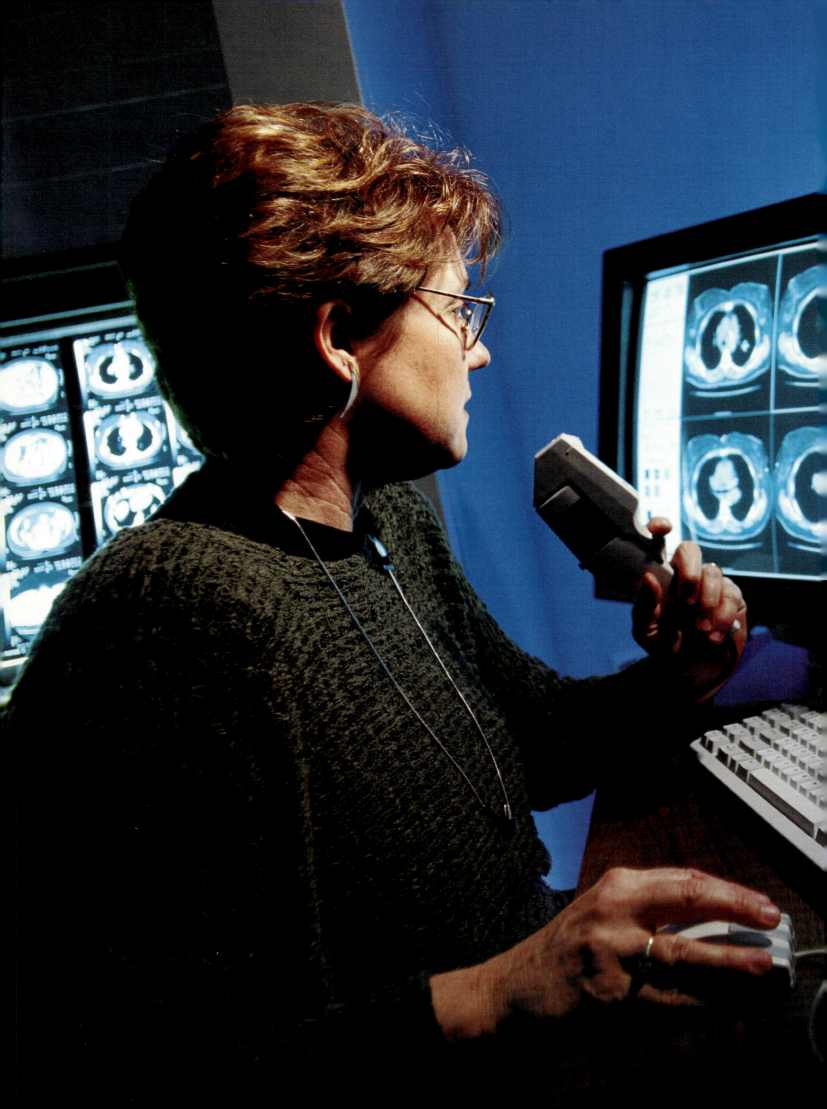

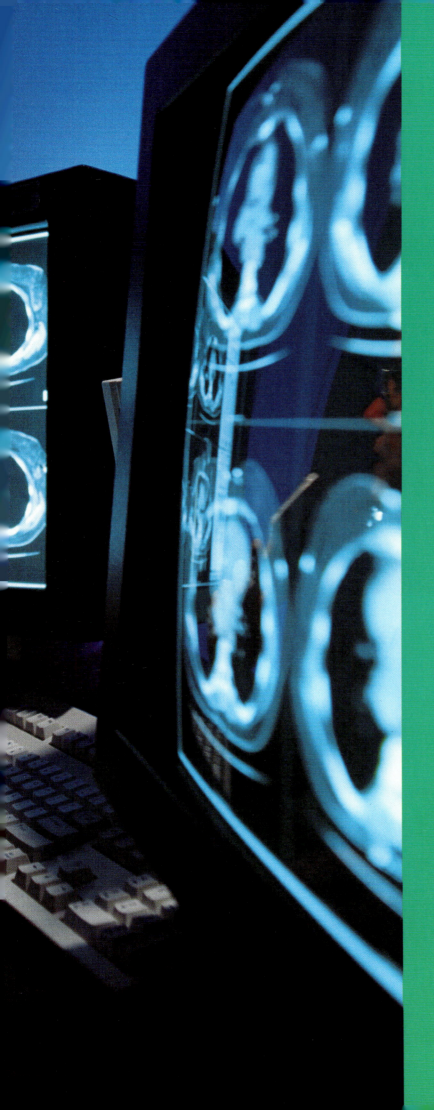

Chapter
Eleven

11

High Technology

From robotics to dot coms to medical engineering, Gainesville's
high-tech industries represent one of the fastest-growing sectors of
the local economy. *Photo by Randy Batista/Media Image*

EXACTECH

Helping people improve their quality of life by maintaining their activity and independence—that is Exactech's founding philosophy and continuing commitment.

Exactech designs, develops, manufactures, and markets orthopaedic implant devices for repair and restoration of human joints. The company also distributes implants for repairing bone fractures and biologic bone repair material to hospitals and surgeons. Exactech's implant devices and biologic allograft material are used to repair damaged bones and joints that have deteriorated due to injury or disease such as arthritis.

Chairman and Chief Executive Officer Bill Petty states, "Exactech's vision is to be the world's leading producer of innovative, high-quality bone and joint restoration products that improve patient outcomes." While that may seem an auda-

■ Exactech's vision is to become the industry leader in production and distribution of bone and joint restoration products. Looking to the future, the company has developed a seven-year forecast of facility requirements; an employee team is evaluating short-term and long-term alternatives for future expansion. Exactech moved into its 38,000-square-foot main building in June of 1998, and in 2000 added a 10,000-square-foot distribution center.

cious goal, the company's history of strong growth and continuing success gives positive indications of an auspicious future. The company has grown steadily over the last five years at a compound annual growth rate of 38 percent. This growth has created an unusually strong following on Wall Street for a firm of Exactech's size. Excellent business fundamentals have earned Exactech recognition

■ Marketing is vital to Exactech's performance. Through its team-based approach, Exactech developed successful marketing plans that enable it to compete effectively in a demanding global marketplace. The company's marketing area is alive with activity as team members carry out their roles in education, promotion, and customer support services.

for two consecutive years as one of *Forbes* magazine's 200 best small companies in America.

Founded in 1985 by Petty who is an orthopaedic surgeon, his wife Betty, and bio-engineer Gary J. Miller, the company quickly began to be recognized for products that made meaningful improvements in solving the problems of joint replacement surgery. After demonstrating several years of solid financial history, Exactech became a publicly traded company on the NASDAQ stock exchange in May of 1996, trading under the symbol EXAC that it also uses for its web address (www.exac.com). In November of 1997, Exactech qualified for certification as an ISO 9001 company. Exactech also earned certification to CE mark its products for acceptance in the European Economic Community. Sales continued to grow both domestically and internationally as Exactech entered markets in Europe, Asia, Australia, and South America.

In 1998, the company built a new facility. It operates out of approximately 50,000 square feet in two buildings located in the Northwood Commercial Park. "Our facility planning team is developing plans for an additional 48,000-square-foot building on our property," said Betty Petty, vice president of administration and human resources. "We need more space as we continually add employees to develop and manufacture new products." Exactech currently employs 130 people in Gainesville. In addition, approximately 125 sales representatives work within independent agencies in the United States to sell Exactech products. Exactech also has distributors in 17 foreign countries. Distribution networks continue to grow in Northern Europe, South America, and Asia.

What are some of Exactech's products and how do these products benefit patients? The AcuMatch® hip line offers excellent range of motion and reduces the likelihood of thigh pain following hip replacement. It also offers a modular hip that covers the full range of complex hip replacement surgeries with a simple system. The Optetrak® knee system features an improved articular geometry that reduces wear of the polyethylene parts, thereby creating a longer-lasting knee reconstruction. The AcuDriver® powered surgical tool aids in the removal of previously implanted prostheses while preserving natural bone when revisions are necessary due to infection or other problems. "The employees of Exactech tell me that they find their work satisfying," says Gary Miller, Ph.D., vice president of research and development and a co-founder of the company. "It's a good feeling to know that what you do when you come to work helps people to be more mobile and have a better quality of life. We are continually looking for ways to find new and better solutions to medical problems that inhibit people's mobility and activity."

Successfully applying the multiple skill sets of many people and fostering their involvement in finding new solutions has played an essential role in the company's success. Exactech uses a team approach to planning. The company's Leadership Team meets regularly to review the company's direction and to measure its progress. Short-term special

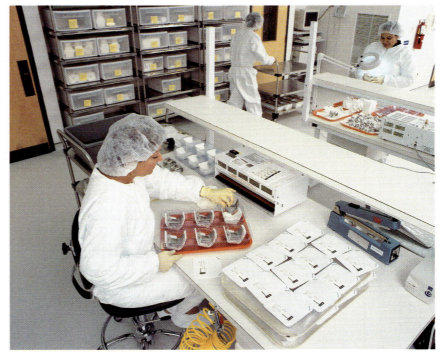

■ Exactech measures its progress in not only lowering costs but in steadily improving its ability to produce the world's most respected joint restoration products. From its inception, Exactech has packaged all its implants, and in recent years it began to produce several of its products in-house, meeting stringent quality standards and FDA regulations.

assignment teams of employees are formed to handle projects ranging from designing a new building to preparing for a major sales and marketing event. The planning process is not merely internal. The company encourages and uses feedback from a wide range of associates including scientists, surgeons, consultants, independent sales associates, and others. "This has created a widespread sense of ownership and sense of shared responsibility for the company's progress that has resulted in a powerful dynamic," says Tim Seese, president and chief operating officer.

Other elements of the company's culture that contribute to its success are dedication to excellence, strong respect for innovation and achievement, the highest ethical standards, belief in the power of empowerment, and caring for the individual.

"Exactech is an organization with a strong sense of community, based on the shared values and vision of its people," says Dr. Petty. "This sense of community extends to our local community—Gainesville, Florida, and throughout the world where we provide benefits with our products and services. At the same time, we develop relationships with, and learn from, people of different backgrounds and cultures. At Exactech, we strive to foster an environment where we can grow both professionally and personally while making contributions that improve lives around the globe." ■

■ Surgeons and bio-engineers lead Exactech's product design efforts. Each product is developed with the company's mission in mind: to improve the quality of life for individuals by maintaining their activity and independence.

BARR SYSTEMS, INC. ────────────

In 1978, Tony Barr took an innovative idea for a file transfer device for computers and invented a company. Barr Systems, a leading provider of mainframe connectivity and print management solutions, began with one programmer's concept of sharing mainframe resources with the personal computer (PC) networking world and translated it into one of Gainesville's largest and most successful companies.

Beginning his pursuit in Raleigh, North Carolina, Barr relocated his business to Gainesville, Florida, in 1985 after the success of his first development, BARR/HASP. This product did something relatively unheard of in the early '80s. It allowed sharing of information (specifically high-volume print jobs) between the immense, previously

■ *Barr's central courtyard shown lighted at night. Photo by Randy Batista*

impenetrable giant of the mainframe to the easily accessible personal computer. Now settled in the heart of beautiful central Florida, Barr quickly grew his business into a multi-million dollar, internationally recognized company and leader in the software development industry.

Through Barr's extensive commitment to quality and order, the company received recognition in product and business excellence. After building a new 52,000-square-foot complex in 1997, the company won even greater acknowledgement for its tropically landscaped corporate campus, designed to offer employees the highest quality working environment. Every employee has a personal office space and a window view. At the center of the Barr campus stands a three-tiered fountain imported from Mexico, surrounded by a pergola, an Italian designed arbor. For two years, Barr won Gainesville's city beautification award for enhancing the local scenery.

But Barr's involvement in the local community hardly stops there. Although its campus provides wooded trails and forest surroundings for residents near its northwest location, it is the activity of employees that really brings prosperity to the Gainesville community. From their efforts in local and national charity events, to their partnership with the University of Florida, the employees of Barr Systems are motivated to enhance and enrich the city in which they live.

Barr Systems may be headquartered in Gainesville, but its business is truly international. Barr serves Fortune 1,000 companies around the globe. These companies rely on Barr Systems' host connectivity and print management software to help them connect, distribute, and print from mainframe bases to branch offices, which are often located thousands of miles away.

As a business that has attained the highest ISO 9000 certification, as well as the designation of Microsoft Certified Solutions Provider, Barr Systems is a world-class corporate force. The future could be even brighter for the 22-year computer veteran. With the advent of the Internet over the last decade, the connectivity experts at Barr Systems will be among the pioneers in the next century to help businesses connect their corporate data sources to the world via the World Wide Web. ■

■ *Entrance to Barr's corporate campus. Photo by Randy Batista*

REGENERATION TECHNOLOGIES, INC. _____

Regeneration Technologies, Inc., (RTI) is one of Gainesville's biggest success stories. A spin-off of the University of Florida Tissue Bank Inc., RTI was founded in 1998 to develop new technology and products using human donor bone and tissue, known as allograft tissue.

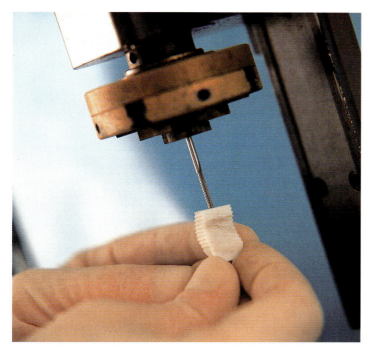

■ RTI develops and precision-tools implants for orthopedic and other surgery.

"At RTI, we expand the gift of tissue donation to the fullest possible extent," said Jamie M. Grooms, RTI chief executive officer. "We precision-tool tissue that becomes allograft implants and is used in orthopedic surgery and urological, vascular, and oral/maxillofacial surgery. In 2000, we helped more than 125,000 people with our products."

The company's growth has been nothing short of phenomenal. In 1998, RTI employed 100. In 2000, as 110,000 additional square feet of office and laboratory space were under construction, almost 400 employees were on the RTI team. When construction is completed, RTI will occupy about 177,000 square feet in Alachua's Progress Corporate Park.

Engineers, scientists, medical specialists, biomedical laboratory technologists, computer programmers/analysts, machinists, tissue processors, national donor recovery specialists, and administrators produce approximately 30 precision-shaped products for health-care professionals throughout the world. Several products are patented or have patents pending.

Besides processing tissue into shaped implants, RTI provides services to hospitals and surgeons—from safe tissue recovery (through its tissue bank partners) to tissue distribution. RTI also processes and distributes common types of tissue, including bone, osteoarticular grafts, tendon, and cartilage. The firm assists with biomedical laboratory testing and provides its tissue bank partners with management consultation services. Research and development of new technologies, like the BioCleanse tissue cleansing system, is a major focus at RTI.

"As baby boomers age, they want to stay active. That is where we can help," said Grooms. RTI's bone paste product, for example, can help bone grow and is used to repair bone chips or gaps caused from injury or deteriorating bone.

To insure safety, all donated tissue goes through rigorous screening, testing, and processing procedures at RTI. Donor tissue is accepted for processing only after donors pass strict disease screening and testing. The donor tissue then undergoes a thorough cleaning and disinfection process and is preserved by freezing or freeze-drying.

"Using bone and tissue has been around for 100 years, but in the last five years we have helped push the technology to the forefront," said Grooms. "We are committed to pushing technology even farther to develop new methods, products, and techniques so patients can heal faster, be more active, and lead more productive lives."

RTI has earned ISO 9001 certification, a quality assurance recognition by the International Standards Organization. The company is traded on the Nasdaq.

In the community, RTI is involved in United Way and the American Heart Walk, and supports increased awareness of tissue donation through the Nick Oelrich golf tournament and the Five Points of Life Bicycle Ride. ■

■ RTI pays careful attention to quality, thoroughly screening and testing all tissue.

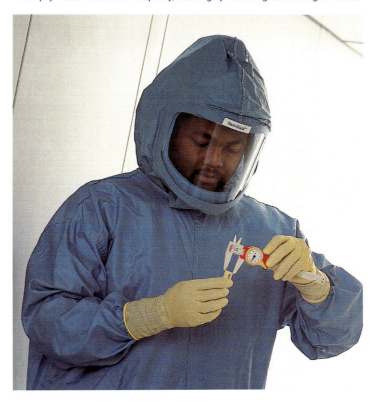

MEDICAL DEVICE TECHNOLOGIES, INC.

Medical Device Technologies, Inc., (MD Tech) is a manufacturer and supplier of specialty needles to hospitals and clinics throughout the world, and one of Gainesville's leading medical manufacturing companies. MD Tech's needles help physicians diagnose and treat various diseases. They are most commonly used in the areas of radiology, radiation oncology, clinical oncology/ hematology, and urology. The company also manufactures specialty catheters, used by interventional radiologists, gynecologists, and urologists. MD Tech's current product list includes more than 600 items.

MD Tech began in 1986 as National Standard Medical Products, Inc., a division of National Standard, Inc., a Michigan-based steel wire manufacturer. The company, created in Gainesville to develop a product invented by a local physician, started manufacturing in a 3,000-square-foot space in Gainesville's Southwest Industrial Park. Its original product was a breast lesion localization needle, used to mark and immobilize tumors of the breast prior to surgical excision.

companies in the United States to be recognized as an ISO 9001 company by the International Standard Organization. Registered and controlled by the Food and Drug Administration, MD Tech operates one of Gainesville's few clean room facilities, where air is carefully regulated and controlled to prevent contamination.

The firm works closely with the physicians who use its products. "We are committed to advancing the technology and developing new products," says Baker. "We constantly seek input and suggestions from our instrument users."

A member of the Gainesville Area Chamber of Commerce and Council for Economic Outreach and United Way supporter, MD Tech is well-established as a community participant. "We are located in Gainesville, in part, because of our ability to conduct research here and because of the well-educated and skilled employees we are able to attract," says Baker. ■

■ MD Tech headquarters.

By 1990, the company became a member of The Marmon Group and changed its name to Medical Device Technologies, Inc., commonly known under its trademark, MD Tech. As the company grew, an additional 16,000 square feet of space was leased in the Southwest Industrial Park. In 1998, MD Tech moved into its current location. The new facility on 47th Avenue, located behind the U.S. Post Office headquarters on SW 34th Street, comprises 42,000 square feet, with enough adjacent land to double the size of the plant as the organization grows.

A staff of 117 employees handles manufacturing, distribution, marketing, and administrative tasks from the Gainesville facility to their major markets in Germany, Japan, Canada, the United Kingdom, Italy, France, Spain, Australia, and the United States.

"In addition to internal development, we have grown through the acquisition of product lines and technologies from other companies," says Paul Baker, MD Tech president.

MD Tech has doubled in size every two years since 1990. The company was one of the first medical

■ State-of-the-art clean room facility.

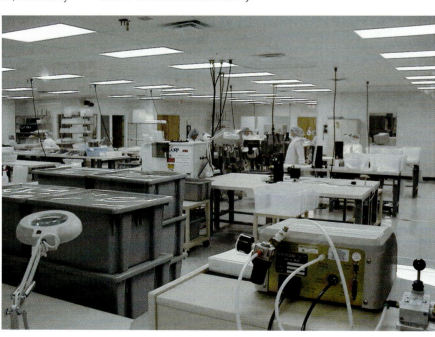

UNIVERSITY OF FLORIDA'S SID MARTIN BIOTECHNOLOGY DEVELOPMENT INCUBATOR

As Florida's only bio-business incubator, the Sid Martin Biotechnology Development Institute (BDI) at the University of Florida is a statewide resource for helping transfer technology based on University of Florida research to the private sector.

■ The BDI's splendid technical and scientific facilities provide a professional environment to jumpstart high-tech enterprises. *Photo by Allen Cheuvront*

"We work with start-up companies as they develop a concept and a technology, then we help them through business plan development, assembly of a management team, securing funding, presentations to venture capitalists, technology development, and finally to commercialization," said Dr. Sheldon M. Schuster, director of the Biotechnology Program at the University of Florida.

The BDI, located in Progress Corporate Park in Alachua, helps new companies move toward profitability by providing state-of-the-art laboratory and office facilities. Wet labs, a greenhouse, a fermentation facility, and shared scientific equipment are available for companies to use, along with a library, audio-visual equipment, a darkroom, walk-in cold rooms and incubator, a small animal containment facility, furnished entrepreneurial offices, and conference rooms.

During the BDI's first five years, 82 percent of the 22 incubator companies are still growing and have raised $25 million in equity and more

■ Common use laboratory and office equipment enables fledgling companies to focus their funds on product development.

than $4 million in grants. Three companies have successfully started independent operations in Alachua County. Two companies attracted buyers and were absorbed into larger companies, and three others left BDI and are still operational. Three additional companies will soon graduate from the BDI and show excellent promise for future success.

"The work of the BDI is a very important component of regional economic development," said Dr. Schuster. "The biotechnology industry has tremendous growth potential for creating high end jobs in our community." In fact, BDI companies have provided 309 full-time equivalent years of employment over the past five years—all at wages well above the Alachua County average.

Companies approved for the BDI negotiate a license fee paid in cash and equity. In return BDI provides access to space, facilities, services, and equipment. Companies generally remain in the incubator for four years, with an option for a fifth year.

BDI companies are involved in an impressive array of projects. One is developing a new way of recycling waste into useful fuels. Another is working on a new class of diagnostic reagents to determine if one has cancer much earlier than previously possible. Still another is working on ways to mitigate plant diseases in crops that have worldwide importance.

"This is truly an opportunity for people to do well and do good at the same time," said Dr. Schuster.

Amid this entire scientific endeavor, the BDI has not neglected its community. "We began working with the community when we built the facility. Community groups hold meetings, conferences, and science fairs here, too," Dr. Schuster said. Art from fifth graders at Alachua Elementary School adorns lobby walls, a symbol of BDI's close relationship with its neighbors. ■

IXION BIOTECHNOLOGY, INC.

Ixion is a biotechnology company focusing on the treatment of metabolic disorders. Creating a world free of diabetes, kidney stones, and other debilitating metabolic diseases is Ixion's goal. Ixion is the world's leader in stem cell-based cellular therapy for diabetes, and diagnostic and preventive options for oxalate-related disorders, such as kidney stones, primary hyperoxaluria, Crohn's Disease, and cystic fibrosis.

Founded in 1993 in Gainesville, Ixion licensed its initial technology from the University of Florida, with whom it enjoys a close relationship. The firm's laboratories and executive offices are located in the heart of North Florida's biotechnology community at the Progress Corporate Park in Alachua. Ixion holds worldwide patents or exclusive licenses in islet stem cells, diabetes, and oxalate-related disorders.

More than 16 million people in the United States have diabetes and 100 million suffer from the disease worldwide. "We are working to cure diabetes and prevent hyperoxaluria and kidney stones," said Weaver H. Gaines, chairman and chief executive officer. "It's all about finding new science to give new hope to people for whom there are no good solutions presently available," he said.

Type 1 diabetes is the most severe form of the disease. Type 1 patients and many type 2 patients must take insulin shots daily. The insulin shots stave off death, but do not cure the disease nor protect against complications such as diabetic coma, insulin shock, renal disease, blindness, amputations, nerve damage, and cardiovascular and periodontal disease.

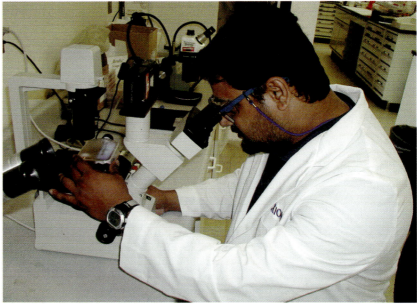

■ Director of Diabetes Research Doctor Vijay Ramiya at microscope.

Ixion's diabetes products are based on its stem cell technology. This technology gives Ixion the ability to propagate and differentiate islet stem cells in test tubes and will provide a source of human islets for use in cell transplantation therapy. The transplantation of islets is the only known potential cure for type 1 diabetes.

Ixion also has several oxalate products in development: a drug for the therapeutic treatment of oxalate-related diseases, a product to prevent kidney stones in companion animals, a diagnostic test for the presence of *Oxalobacter formigenes*, and an oxalate-resistant catheter for urinary applications. Using the same technology, Ixion could also formulate a nutritional supplement to promote healthy levels of oxalate.

Kidney stones affect about one million patients annually. There are 1,500 patients with primary hyperoxaluria, a rare, usually fatal disease; 25,000 cystic fibrosis patients are affected by excess oxalate.

In 2000, the Small Business Administration awarded Ixion the National Tibbetts Award. This award is given to a select group of small firms, projects, organizations, or individuals judged to exemplify the best in achievement by the Small Business Innovation Research Program. Ixion was one of only two winners in Florida and 56 nationwide.

To learn more about Ixion Biotechnology, Inc., the company encourages you to visit its Web site at www.ixion-biotech.com or call its headquarters at 386-418-1428. ■

■ Director of Oxalate Research Doctor Harmeet Sidhu.

12

Chapter Twelve

Business and Finance

In Gainesville, the numbers add up to economic vitality. Together, the city's business and financial institutions form the pulse of Gainesville's thriving economy. *Photo by Ray Carson*

GAINESVILLE AREA CHAMBER OF COMMERCE

In 1995, Money magazine named Gainesville the number one best place to live in the United States. The magazine cited this "picturesque area as one of the few places in the U.S. where someone can work in town, live in the country, and have a maximum 30-minute commute." Thanks to the work of the Gainesville Area Chamber of Commerce (GACC) over the past 75 years, Gainesville is still "the best place to live in the U.S!"

■ Improving local education is an important goal for the Gainesville Area Chamber of Commerce. Each year, the Chamber holds a ProEd Golf Classic to raise money for their Teacher Mini-Grants Program, through which area teachers may apply for grants worth up to $250. 2000 Community Improvement Vice Chair Kevin Smith presents Duval Elementary School with a mini-grant.

"Our chamber has been a driving force in helping to keep Gainesville prosperous and still preserve our wonderful quality of life," said Marilyn Tubb, 1999 and 2000 Chamber chair.

For 75 years The Gainesville Area Chamber of Commerce has worked to improve the community and make Gainesville and Alachua County an ideal place to live and operate a business.

"When I came back to Gainesville after World War II, the Chamber was just a little group of people downtown who were interested in moving the Chamber forward with economic development," remembers M. M. Parrish, one of the Chamber's first presidents.

After the Chamber began an effort to enhance economic development, a strong foundation was laid by locating businesses including North American Archery Group, North Florida Regional Medical Center, Metal Container Corporation, and Florida Farm Bureau Federation. The Chamber's sister organization, the Gainesville Council for Economic Outreach (CEO), has built on that foundation of success with employers including Dollar General, Nordstrom, Exactech, and MD Tech.

According to Tubb, those new businesses represent jobs, an important ingredient for any thriving community. "Bringing new business to Gainesville and helping our

homegrown businesses grow is vital to our health and prosperity. A healthy business community translates into better schools, a lower crime rate, and a more prosperous community through higher paying jobs for all our citizens."

Indeed the Chamber's mission is to "provide advocacy, services, and information to enhance economic opportunity in our community," by working with a diverse group of businesses, local and state government, and community leaders.

The Chamber and CEO are members of the Alliance for Economic Development, created to help coordinate activities more strategically and aggressively, according to Alliance President Bob Rohrlack.

"In a community like Gainesville, we have a narrow tax base because of our large number of government agencies," says Rohrlack. "That's why it is so important for us to build business and for businesses to partner with other community groups," he said.

From 1994 to 2000, CEO helped create more than 2,600 new jobs in the community and add more than $5 million in tax revenue by assisting existing businesses with expansion efforts and attracting new professional, manufacturing, and distribution firms to the area.

Numerous organizations have been created from Chamber committees and initiatives, including the East Gainesville Development Task Force,

■ The Chamber believes that companies prefer to do business with people they know and provides various opportunities for members to network with other members. Each month the Chamber holds Chamber After Hours, an event designed to bring members in contact with each other in a casual setting. Attendance at these events is close to 300 every month.

■ The Gainesville Area Chamber of Commerce has been an integral part of the community for almost 77 years. In 1999, the Chamber held an anniversary annual meeting to celebrate 75 years of success. Pictured from left are past Chamber presidents Betsy Whitaker (1982), Scott Medley (1997), M. M. Parrish, Jr. (1955), Judy Boles (1994), Howard Hall (1963), Robert Woody (1998), and Mark Walker (1995).

a group working to help East Gainesville prosper, and the Gainesville Sports Organizing Committee, an organization that helps bring sporting events to Gainesville. The Partners in Education program, another Chamber spin-off, has raised more than $1.4 million in donations and in-kind contributions to the Alachua County School Board from area businesses. In fact, working with area schools is a major Chamber focus. "Our members communicate regularly with our school leaders so we can help them develop classes, improve our schools, and cooperatively work to train our young people to become productive employees in our community," says Tubb.

One of the Chamber's most important programs is Leadership Gainesville, the nation's fourth oldest community leadership development program. More than 1,000 have graduated from the six-month course in the past 26 years. Participants learn about the business and local community through social services, law enforcement, education, agriculture, medicine, and the arts. The Leadership Gainesville Alumni Association has underwritten the "Kid-Start Program," which donates school supplies, backpacks, and shirts to hundreds of Head-Start children in the county each year.

The Chamber has also been a leader in coordinating visits to other cities to help bring a community vision to Gainesvllle. Members and elected officials share new ideas and learn better ways to help Gainesville grow and prosper.

The Chamber is 1,300-plus members strong and represents some 65,000 employees in those businesses. Interestingly, the bulk of the Chamber's members are small

businesses, with fewer than 25 employees. "We provide tremendous benefits to these folks, from marketing advice to seminars, workshops, and of course networking opportunities," said Tubb.

In fall 2001, the Chamber will move into the new Commerce Center in downtown Gainesville. The new building will house the Chamber, CEO, and the Alliance, along with like-minded economic development organizations. A boardroom will be available to community groups, along with facilities to handle meetings for 300-plus people.

"This is really a step to move us to the next level," says Rohrlack. "This new facility will show the community the importance of the business community and where these organizations are going. None of this would be possible without our members and the city helping to make it happen," he said.

It's no wonder Gainesville has been named an "All America City" (1971), a "best place to live in America" (1994-98), and a "best place to raise an outdoor family" (*Outdoor Explorer*, 1999), and is home to the University of Florida, one of the "best universities in the U.S." (*U.S. News and World Report*, 1999), Shands Hospital, "one of the best hospitals in America" (*U.S. News and World Report*, 1999), and North Florida Regional Medical Center, "100 Top Hospitals™: National Benchmarks for Success—2000" (HCIA-Sachs)! Visit Gainesville and see why it is such a great place to live and one of the best places to grow a business. ■

■ In 2001, the Chamber will move into its new offices in the Commerce Center, located at 300 East University Avenue in downtown Gainesville. The Center will also house the Florida Community Design Center, a community development and resource center. The Design Center will promote the practice of good community design in the built and natural environment in Gainesville, Alachua County, and the State of Florida.

CAMPUS USA CREDIT UNION _____

*F*or more than 65 years, CAMPUS USA Credit Union has served members in the Gainesville area. Originally chartered in 1935 to serve employees, faculty, and staff of the University of Florida, CAMPUS now serves a three-county area and members all over the world.

"This has been a time of tremendous growth for us," Larry Scott, president and chief executive officer said. "As we grow and add new members and locations, we will be able to continue to offer innovative and low-cost or free services to our members."

Today, CAMPUS operates as a member-directed, member-owned non-profit cooperative. Anyone who lives, works, or attends school in Alachua, Marion, or Columbia counties is eligible to join the credit union. As a member-owned cooperative, profits are distributed to members each year in the form of best of market rates on loans and deposits and low-cost financial services.

CAMPUS deposits come equipped with the highest level of insurance protection available. In addition to $100,000 in federal deposit insurance provided by the National Credit Union Administration, up to $250,000 in private deposit insurance is also provided by Excess Share Insurance, a wholly owned subsidiary of ASI, the nation's largest private deposit insurer. The additional coverage is free of charge to any CAMPUS member whose account requires it, so each member is covered for up to $350,000.

CAMPUS will also match or beat any competitor's rate on loans. Lending services include new and used auto loans; first and second mortgages; home equity, recreational vehicle, boat, and motorcycle loans; and credit cards from Visa and MasterCard. CAMPUS home loans offer 15-, 20-, and 30-year terms with guaranteed lowest closing costs.

■ (Above) Serving Gainesville since 1935, CAMPUS USA stands as the largest locally owned financial institution in the area.

■ (Below) Local management ensures that CAMPUS can adapt to local market conditions. As a result, CAMPUS members enjoy best of market rates on loans and deposits.

Banking with CAMPUS is easy and inexpensive. Locations can be found throughout Gainesville including East Campus at 1200 SW 5th Avenue; West Campus at 1900 SW 34th Street; Hunters Crossing at 200 NW 43rd Street; Tower Square at 5725 SW 75th Street; Shands at UF in Room H-1; the Delta Center at 2511 NW 41st Street; and Springhills Commons shopping center near the intersection of I-75 and NW 39th Avenue. A new location was opened in early 2001 in Ocala on SR 200 across from the Paddock Mall.

CAMPUS also provides walk-up Automated Teller Machine (ATM) Services. Drive-up ATMs are available at the East Campus, West Campus, and Springhills locations. Members can use their ATM card or Visa CheckCard to access any CAMPUS, "CU 24 CU Here," or Publix Presto! ATM free of charge.

Members also have the convenience of banking at home with CAMPUS' electronic banking services. Through its Web site at www.campuscu.com, the credit union provides CAMPUS QUE online banking services. Account information is also available by phone through CAMPUS CALL. All services are free of charge for CAMPUS members.

CAMPUS supports key community programs in Gainesville. One charity the credit union has been heavily involved with is the Children's Miracle Network (CMN) and Shands Children's Hospital. In partnership with Shands, CAMPUS launched the CMN Visa. The card, with one of the lowest fixed interest rates in the country at 9.8 percent, generates donations to CMN when a cardholder makes any retail purchase. A portion of the interchange fee that the credit union

■ Service makes a difference in financial services. CAMPUS' staff is trained to offer the highest level of personalized member service.

■ CAMPUS is delivering the latest technologies to members at the lowest cost possible. Most CAMPUS services, like Internet banking, are free to members.

receives from merchants who accept the card is donated directly to the Children's Hospital via CMN. In 2000, the card raised more than $30,000 in donations with that number expected to increase as more members take the card.

Other community organizations that benefit from CAMPUS' participation include the American Cancer Society's "Relay for Life" event, the United Way of Alachua County, and the Alachua County School Board Foundation's "Take Stock in Children" program. CAMPUS also sponsors local athletic teams including the University of Florida Gators.

Scott is proud of CAMPUS and thinks members should be too.

"Our members are what make everything possible here at CAMPUS," Scott said. "They are the fuel that keeps us running, allowing us to give back to Gainesville. I believe we all share in the credit union's success, and I think our members know that."

The credit union is the largest locally owned and operated financial institution in the Gainesville area, with more than 70,000 members and more than $400 million in total assets. CAMPUS USA Credit Union is an Equal Housing Lender. The company employs 150. ■

TOWER HILL INSURANCE GROUP

Motivated by the desire to find a better place to raise a family, Tower Hill Insurance Group's Chief Executive Officer, William J. Shively, moved his fledgling company from Miami to Gainesville in 1981. At that time the company was known as Mobile Home Insurance Associates.

■ Tower Hill's Gainesville Corporate Headquarters.

In Gainesville, Shively found not only a community well suited for children and families, but also one that provided a firm foundation for growth and prosperity for the company that would eventually be known as Tower Hill Insurance Group. Since moving to Gainesville, Tower Hill has grown from five employees to more than 400 employees. Today the company occupies more than 120,000 square feet of office space. In 2001, Tower Hill was named the sixth largest private employer in Alachua County by *The Gainesville Sun*.

In the insurance industry Tower Hill is known as a Managing General Agency (MGA). As a multi-dimensional MGA, Tower Hill contracts with various insurance companies to manage the product development, marketing, underwriting, policy issuance, and claims adjudication on behalf of the contracted insurer. All of the insurance companies represented by Tower Hill are highly rated by leading independent review companies. Insurers represented by Tower Hill include the companies of the Clarendon Insurance Group, the AXA Corporate Solutions Group, Omega Insurance Company, and the Tower Hill-owned Regency Insurance Company.

Tower Hill focuses on the development, distribution, and management of personal insurance policies

■ Reception area for Tower Hill's unique training center.

including homeowners, mobile homeowners, condominium owners, renters, low value dwelling, automobile, and personal umbrella policies. Today, Tower Hill creates and distributes these policies in 13 states throughout the United States. Sales are made through a network of 2,500 independent insurance agents who write insurance policies for more than 650,000 Tower Hill policyholders. In 1994, the firm wrote $20 million in personal lines premium. In 2000, Tower Hill wrote $440 million of personal lines premium. By 2003, the firm is expected to reach the $1 billion mark in national sales. In addition to the Gainesville headquarters office, Tower Hill currently has offices in Freeport, Maine; Atlanta, Georgia; and Jackson, Mississippi.

Interestingly enough, it was a major catastrophe, Hurricane Andrew that played an integral role in Tower Hill's growth. When Andrew hit South Florida in August of 1992, many insurance companies were financially decimated due to the unprecedented volume of claims they received. Tower Hill was an exception to this scenario due to a well-managed strategy of limiting concentrations of policies in any given area. Tower Hill was able to come through Hurricane Andrew with flying colors. In fact, Tower Hill's primary market in 1992, Omega Insurance Company, actually made a profit that year. Many insurance companies eventually left Florida after Hurricane Andrew and Tower Hill seized this opportunity to expand its premium writings throughout the state.

Today, Tower Hill is particularly proud of its Catastrophe Response Team. The team is a select member of the Florida Department of Insurance's Insurance Disaster Assessment Team. The team is equipped with emergency response vehicles, digital phones, and laptop computers.

The goal of the team is to be on-site within 24 hours of an emergency event. The team is prepared for a Hurricane Andrew-type storm.

Tower Hill's employees are a key ingredient to the overall success of the company. Each Tower Hill employee receives an excellent compensation package that includes a wide array of benefit options, a bonus/incentive program, and a retirement program. In addition, outstanding employees are recognized for their superior program efforts and accomplishments on a quarterly basis. Finally, the Tower Hill Employee of the Year qualifies to travel with other company representatives on the Emerald Circle trip. The Emerald Circle award trip recognizes Tower Hill's top producing agents on an annual basis and membership in the Emerald Circle has climbed to nearly 100 agencies.

Both employees and agents benefit from an extensive training and development program designed by Tower Hill. The Tower Hill Training Department provides training and education in a wide variety of insurance disciplines for employees as well as providing continuing education and licensing courses for Tower Hill agents and their agency staff members.

Tower Hill supports many charitable organizations in Gainesville and Alachua County through the contributions and volunteer efforts of its employees and the Tower Hill Charitable Foundation. Beneficiaries have included the Ronald McDonald House, the Alachua County School District, and numerous other worthwhile causes and organizations.

For more than 20 years Gainesville and Tower Hill have been great partners. The next 20 years promise to be even better! ■

■ Welcome to Tower Hill!—Tower Hill's Corporate Reception Area.

NATIONWIDE INSURANCE _____

*I*n 2000, Nationwide Insurance's Gainesville Customer Service Center celebrated its 20th anniversary. "It has been tremendously rewarding to be a member of this vibrant community," said Michelle Premo, associate vice president of the center. "The combination of Gainesville's labor force of more than 100,000 people with diverse backgrounds, skills, and experience, coupled with an equally strong educational system has contributed significantly to our success."

■ Gainesville Service Center.

In fact, it was these same factors that were used by local business leaders to attract Nationwide to Gainesville. When the company finally broke ground in the late 1970s, the community considered it a major accomplishment and looked with anticipation to what Nationwide would offer its citizens in the coming years.

Nationwide is a Fortune 500 organization with assets of more than $100 billion. Combined, the insurance companies have more than 16 million policies and certificates in force and are served by more than 35,000 employees and agents. Nationwide is one of the largest diversified financial insurance providers in the United States, headquartered in Columbus, Ohio, where the company was founded in 1925. The company is guided by a vision that emphasizes customer service, excellence, ethics, diversity, results, creativity, and teamwork. Its brand tenets—access, customization, and ease of use—mirror its vision. Nationwide offers insurance protection to address most consumer needs, including auto, boat, homeowners, business, as well as life and financial products. Consumer sales are marketed through a number of different mechanisms, some examples are exclusive agents, internet, affinity relationships, banks, and direct marketing-telephone sales.

Nationwide's Gainesville Customer Service Center has grown significantly since officially opening its doors in March of 1980. Originally, a staff of 550 was located in the center and covered a three-state area. Today, the center employs 1,100 serving customers in 13 states, including Florida. The center is organized into three primary service areas: policy-related, claims adjusting/handling, and claims reporting, with an emphasis on auto, homeowners, and business insurance customers. Life, health, and financial products are serviced out of Ohio. Policy-type services include eligibility, coverages, and underwriting, as well as addressing questions related to premiums, billings, and payment plans. These services are offered to customers in six states: Alabama, Delaware, District of Columbia, Florida, Georgia, and Maryland. The claims operation involves adjusting and payment, subrogation and salvage, evaluation of medical fees charged, as well as a number of attorneys who assist with settling claims. The majority of claims adjusting and associated payment involves accidents/mishaps occurring in the state of Florida. The center is also home to a 24-hour, 7 days a week, claims call center where customers from 13 states call to report their claims. Besides these three core functions, the center also includes a variety of support services that cover the physical plant (maintenance, security, sanitation), human resources, training, accounting, mail services, systems, and telecommunications technology.

As a result of the Gainesville Customer Service Center's wide range of operations, there are numerous career opportunities supported by work schedules aimed to fit a variety of needs. "Creating a positive balance between work and family is important, as is a diverse work force," said Premo. An employee activities organization called VOICE (Volunteers of Internal and Community Events) also works to support the balance between work and family and sponsors a number of events throughout the year specifically aimed toward associates and their families.

Another important element of the service center is community involvement. Center associates are extremely proud of Gainesville and the surrounding communities and have found numerous ways to serve and give something back. Some key areas of focus include:

- United Way: Employees raise money every year to support health and human service agencies in Alachua County, with each dollar raised supplemented by a dollar from the Nationwide Foundation.
- Habitat for Humanity: Nationwide funded the cost for the construction of a home, with Nationwide employees donating their weekends to help build it. Employees also recycle aluminum cans with proceeds donated to Habitat.
- March of Dimes: Center employees raise funds throughout the year and participate in the annual walk-a-thon.
- Junior Achievement: Employees participate in the annual bowl-a-thon to raise funds to support school programming. They also donate their time and serve as classroom volunteers teaching Junior Achievement programs.
- Civic Action Program: This is an internal Service Center organization that is aimed toward helping employees increase their political awareness and recognize the importance of voting.
- Education: The Service Center routinely donates computers to Alachua County Schools (more than 1,200 have been donated as of 2000).

The Nationwide Gainesville Service Center is proud to be a member of the Gainesville community and believes that a portion of its success can definitely be attributed to its location and the support from the people who live in it.

For more information about Nationwide, visit the company's Web site at www.nationwide.com. ■

■ (Above) Claims Call Center.

■ (Below) Commercial Customer Service.

■ (Below) Personal Lines Customer Service.

TECHNOLOGY ENTERPRISE CENTER OF GAINESVILLE/ALACHUA COUNTY

The 2001 opening of Gainesville's $2.6 million Technology Enterprise Center (GTEC) signaled a major commitment by the City of Gainesville and Alachua County and the US Department of Commerce Economic Development Administration to help nurture and grow technology start-up companies in the community.

■ The recently constructed Technology Enterprise Center is helping to revitalize the Gainesville Enterprise Zone.

Heralded as one of the best-researched and well-conceived incubator projects in the country, Gainesville's project was four years in the making.

"Our research showed that the incubators with the greatest chance for success are those without real-estate debt," said Conchi Ossa, Economic Development Director for the City and project manager. When construction commenced in early 2000, the land had been

■ GTEC's flexible office spaces allow tenants to tailor their work areas.

donated; federal, city, and county grants had been raised for construction; and many local businesses had donated materials and substantial discounts of labor and products to make GTEC's opening debt-free.

"The city has committed to providing operating subsidies until the facility is self-sufficient," said Ossa. The project is expected to achieve a breakeven financial position in less than five years through rents and service fees charged to tenants. Another key to making Gainesville's incubator successful has been the securing of a major anchor tenant, Cenetec LLC, an independent firm that helps pioneering entrepreneurs turn internet and related technologies into successful companies. Cenetec rents the second floor and part of the first floor of GTEC.

Construction of the 30,000-square-foot, two-story facility was truly a community project according to Ossa. "When we began the project, we decided to design an energy efficient building and use as many local materials as possible," she says. When the project team researched materials, they found that a local manufacturer, American Polysteel Forms, made an energy efficient wall construction product that was perfect for the building. Interestingly, American Polysteel was recruited to Gainesville a few years ago by the Council for Economic Outreach, which is funded by the city and county to operate a countywide economic development business recruitment program. "Polysteel was a wonderful corporate citizen. They gave the city a sizeable discount on materials and worked closely with Paul Stresing, the project's

■ The expansive and bright lobby adds a sense of grandure to the center's entrepreneurial spirit.

architect, and R. O. Camp Construction, Inc., to build the first EPA Energy Star commercial building in Gainesville," said Ossa.

Why has the idea of an incubator been so well received by local government officials? "Eighty percent of all new inventions are created by small business," said Morris Windhorst, director of the Center. "Add to that the fact that most jobs are now created by small business. About 87 percent of companies that graduate from incubators succeed, and 84 percent of those remain in the community for five to ten years." Windhorst adds that the exact opposite is true for new businesses developed outside incubators as 80 percent have failed by their fifth year. "As far as a return on investment, technology incubators are great economic development tools, returning to the community about five dollars for every dollar spent on incubating businesses," said Windhorst.

How does a new business gain admission to the Technology Enterprise Center? First, a company must meet strict eligibility requirements. The business must show that it has a technology, product, or service with a technical advantage over competitors. It must be able to reach optimal revenue levels, create jobs, and graduate from the GTEC within three years. Eligible businesses must have a written business plan and demonstrate that the owners and key personnel possess technical savvy, integrity, dedication, and commitment. Finally, the business must show team-building potential and willingness to accept guidance and participate in an environment of cooperation.

Gainesville City Manager Wayne Bowers is enthusiastic about GTEC's ability to help grow new local companies. "A successful business incubation program can achieve some important economic development goals for a community by generating high-wage jobs for local residents and diversifying the industrial sectors of the area's economy," said Bowers.

Once a business has qualified for admission into GTEC, it is assisted in almost every area of business development and growth. Office space, laboratory, and product assembly areas are available to incubator businesses. All tenant companies share a business library and resource center, conference rooms, employee lounge, outdoor patio, shipping and receiving area, lobby, and secured entry. Educational seminars, one-on-one management assistance, and access to a broad network of community organizations and professional services are also available.

The facility also offers a number of fee-based services such as secretarial and word processing support, special equipment and supplies, and telecommunications and Internet connections through GRUCom.

Another important benefit of GTEC tenancy is access to expertise from the University of Florida. "From the beginning, the University of Florida has been a strong supporter of this project, and we are eager for tenant companies to be able to tap into the expertise and technology of the university," said Ossa. Santa Fe Community College's Center for Business and Professional Development will also help GTEC companies with staff training and development.

The GTEC is located on Hawthorne Road in East Gainesville, an area targeted for redevelopment. "With the Alachua County Sheriff's Office, the new city-county communications center, the new health department, and GTEC, we have attracted a critical mass of workers to this area to help develop more retail and services for the eastside," said Bowers. GTEC businesses will also enjoy tax benefits associated with location in the City of Gainesville's Enterprise Zone. ■

■ Tenant amenities include training sessions and specialized business assistance.

DELL GRAHAM, ATTORNEYS AT LAW _____

*L*ife-size photographs of 1930-era Gainesville greet guests to the lobby of Dell Graham, Attorneys at Law. The photos only hint of the firm's rich history in the Gainesville community. "We're proud of the very deep roots we have in this community," says partner John D. Jopling. "Our firm, which dates back to the turn of the last century, has grown up with many of our clients, here in Gainesville."

Although steeped in local history through its representation of major Gainesville organizations such as Florida Farm Bureau, Nationwide Insurance, State Farm Insurance, the School Board of Alachua County, the City of Gainesville, Shands HealthCare, North Florida Regional Medical Center, the University of Florida College of Medicine, and many individuals and businesses—Dell Graham is now a rather young firm in terms of ages of its attorneys and its up-to-the-minute knowledge and use of today's constantly changing technology.

"All our case management is computerized—from timekeeping to our on-line library," says partner Carl B. Schwait. "Our use of these technologies is in keeping with our firm's mission," says Schwait. That mission is to provide zealous, skilled, and cost-effective advocacy of our clients' interests while adhering to the highest standards of professional ethics.

■ Partners and Associates of Dell Graham.

■ Senior Partners of Dell Graham, from left: John D. Jopling, Ellen R. Gershow, and Carl B. Schwait.

Dell Graham provides representation in both general practice and civil litigation with a major emphasis in the insurance industry. Other practice specialties include estate planning, business tax, and organizational law. The firm has extensive trial experience in both state and federal courts through North Central Florida.

The firm has produced circuit and appellate judges as well as leaders of the local bar. Distinguished alumni of the firm include S. T. Dell, L. William Graham, Joe C. Willcox, and W. Henry Barber, Jr. Firm members and employees are also involved in the Gainesville community, outside the legal system. From teaching at the University of Florida Levin College of Law, to active participation in local charities, civic groups, and places of worship, Dell Graham endeavors to give back to the community it is proud to call home.

Attorneys of the firm are senior partners: John D. Jopling, Carl B. Schwait, and Ellen R. Gershow; partner: David A. Cornell; and associates: David M. Delaney, Donna M. Keim, Dale J. Paleschic, and Elizabeth M. Collins. ■

COMPASS BANK

*C*ompass Bank came to the Gainesville community in January 1998, when it acquired Gainesville State Bank. *The bank now has five area branches in Gainesville and one in Ocala—all offering a full range of financial and banking services.*

"We're very proud of the fact that we retain local control right here in Gainesville," says Rafael Bustillo, city president and regional executive officer. "Compass gives us full autonomy to operate as a community bank so we can build relationships and give personalized customer service. We really have the best of both worlds. We make decisions locally, but are able to take advantage of a wide range of national products and services, at highly competitive rates," he said.

S. Clark Butler, former chairman of the board of Gainesville State Bank, is an active director with Compass Bank.

"Our firm, Butler Enterprises, continues to do business with the bank," says Butler. "After Compass came to town, people learned that Compass was efficient and served the public well. In fact it could serve in a much larger capacity than a local bank—in terms of commercial loans and other services."

Bustillo is proud of the role Compass takes in local community activities. "We believe in being an active contributor," he says. Organizations supported by Compass include the American Heart Association, American Cancer Society, Santa Fe Community College, Take Stock in Children, United Way, Harn Museum, Children's Home Society, University of Florida's Phillips Center for Performing Arts, March of Dimes, STOP! Children's Cancer, and the Competitive Edge program of the Gainesville Council for Economic Outreach, among others.

Bustillo credits the Compass staff for making the bank the success it is today. "We are truly fortunate to have such high quality officers and staff on our local team," he says.

■ *Photo by Randy Batista, Media Image Photography*

At the corporate level, Compass Bank was founded in 1964 in Birmingham, Alabama, as Central Bank and Trust. Today, Compass Bank is among the top 40 U.S. bank holding companies by asset size and among the top earners in size based on return on equity. A Sun Belt financial holding company, Compass has assets of over $20 billion and operates 340 full-service banking offices in seven states: Alabama, Arizona, Colorado, Florida, Nebraska, New Mexico, and Texas.

For the fourth consecutive year, Compass was named to the honor roll of Keefe, Bruyette, and Woods, Inc. (KBW), a New York investment banking firm, specializing in financial services. The honor roll designation recognizes Compass as one of the best performing banks over the last decade. Compass was one of just 13 recognized nationally. KBW tracks 138 companies throughout the United States.

Compass Bank holds Moody's Investors Service "Dividend Achiever Designation," an award that recognizes companies that have increased stockholder dividends for 10 consecutive years. Compass was also named to *Forbes Magazine's* "Platinum 400" list as one of the best big companies in America. ■

■ *Photo by Randy Batista, Media Image Photography*

Chapter Thirteen

Building Greater Gainesville

Gainesville has experienced steady economic growth, even during times of national unemployment and fiscal insecurity. Technology centers, retail outlets, office complexes, and literally hundreds of new housing units from student apartments to private-access mansions are under construction at any given time. The last three years saw an unprecedented accelerated pace of commercial and residential development. Among the new construction is the three-story, 65,000-square-foot Commerce Building at 300 East University Avenue. The Gainesville Area Chamber of Commerce will occupy about half of the first floor. *Photo by Randy Batista/Media Image*

LEGACY AT FORT CLARKE

One of Gainesville's newest and most elegant apartment communities, Legacy at Fort Clarke, is a 444-unit luxury community located off Newberry Road on Fort Clarke Boulevard. Legacy at Fort Clarke opened in June 1999 and offers a host of amenities including: privacy fencing with gated access, lush and extensive landscaping, 24-hour resident business center, state-of-the-art fitness center, tropical outdoor swimming pool, lighted tennis and basketball courts, sand volleyball court, children's playground, several car-care centers, picnic and barbecue areas, and laundry facilities. Optional garages, carports, and storage facilities are available within the community.

■ Legacy at Fort Clark's commitment to preserving the natural beauty of the Gainesville landscape is evident to everyone entering this tasteful apartment community.

All apartments are richly detailed with quality craftsmanship and come equipped with intrusion alarms, ceramic tiled foyers, kitchens and baths, nine-foot ceilings, built-in bookcases, decorator glass shelves, custom European-style cabinetry, six-panel doors, ceiling fans, spacious closets, screened patios, and full-size washer and dryer connections.

One-, two-, three-, and four-bedroom apartment homes are available in seven different floor plans to suit any individual or family need. Apartments range in size from 784 square feet in the efficiently planned one-bedroom, one-bathroom Harrision model to the spacious Westcott model, which is four-bedrooms, two baths and includes 1,456 square feet of luxury. All floor plans include oversized bedroom closets and pantries in all kitchens.

Legacy at Fort Clarke has preserved the natural attributes that gave Gainesville its famed reputation as the "Tree City." "We worked very hard to keep this beautiful property as pristine as possible," said Sydney Peters, property manager. "We wanted to create a style of living that was

not typical in Gainesville. We wanted to create a prestigious location with a diverse mix of residents in one of Gainesville's most beautiful locations," she said.

Explore 55 acres of Legacy's nature trails, nestled in the northwest sector of Gainesville. Legacy at Fort Clarke is situated in a serene environment with beautiful canopied trees and majestic pines dotting the landscape. Among the natural landscape one will find picnic areas scattered throughout, much like a park.

Domestic pets up to 80 pounds are welcome at Legacy at Fort Clarke. There's even a doggie playground just for them. Pets require a small deposit and each resident may have up to two pets per apartment.

Legacy at Fort Clarke's location is just minutes from Gainesville's most popular shopping center, the Oaks Mall, right off Interstate 75. Grocery stores and the University of Florida campus are nearby, along with excellent schools (Hidden Oak Elementary, Fort Clarke Middle School, and Buchholz High School) and the nationally known medical services of Shands HealthCare, North Florida Regional Medical Center, and the Veteran's Administration Hospital.

For those looking for social activities, Legacy at Fort Clarke has plenty to offer. Residents enjoy holiday themed parties, pool parties,

■ The spacious and well-appointed clubhouse is the perfect spot for the various types of social activities offered at Legacy Fort Clark.

■ One of the most beautiful and luxurious amenities afforded Legacy at Fort Clark residents is the tropical outdoor swimming pool.

multi-family real estate firms. Trammell Crow Residential has locations in more than 50 United States cities. In Florida, Trammell Crow Residential has properties in Orlando, Destin, Tampa, and South Florida. The firm is dedicated to developing, acquiring, constructing, and managing apartment communities of the highest quality standards, to enhance the lifestyles of residents and create value for investors.

Legacy at Fort Clarke is a member of the Gainesville Area Chamber of Commerce, the Gainesville Apartment Association, Civitan Regional Blood Bank, and sponsors a football team for the local Boy's and Girl's Club.

Trammel Crow Residential offers several unique programs that are available to Legacy at Fort Clarke residents. For example, all residents are guaranteed that if for some reason they need to break their lease within the first 30 days, there will be no penalty. Another is the 24-hour maintenance guarantee. If there is no response to a service request within 24 hours, rent is reduced for each additional day before the service is provided. Trammell Crow Residential and Legacy at Fort Clarke are committed to looking out for residents' best interests. ■

and barbecues with entertainment and catered food. There are also a host of special activities for children.

Another Legacy at Fort Clarke feature is its corporate housing, available through ExecuStay by Marriott. Whether a businessperson is in town for extended meetings or moving to town and needing a place to stay for a short period, the ExecuStay program may be just what they are looking for. All apartments are leased for a minimum of three months and include professionally decorated and furnished interiors. All utilities, cable, phone, and weekly maid service are included along with a TV, VCR, microwave, and answering machine. Kitchens are fully stocked and all linens are supplied, as well.

Moving into Legacy at Fort Clarke includes a welcome package with special offers from local businesses and information about area services. Restaurant, entertainment, and fitness center discounts are available for all Legacy at Fort Clarke residents.

The fitness center at Legacy is a popular place for working out and toning. Precor machines are available to help runners with bad knees. "Precor burns more calories per minute than any other machine to date," said Peters. Treadmills, stair climbers, recumbent bicycles, and leverage weight machines are available, along with a full-body circuit training line. There is also a television and playroom for children.

Legacy at Fort Clarke's management team is always there to serve and assist residents. "We are proud of our professional staff here at Legacy. They are dedicated to top-quality and friendly service," said Peters.

Legacy at Fort Clarke is owned and managed by Trammell Crow Residential, one of America's premier

■ Other amenities include a state-of-the-art fitness center, lighted tennis and basketball courts, a 24-hour resident business center, several car-care centers, a children's playground (shown here), and much more.

CHARLES PERRY CONSTRUCTION INC. ───────────

For more than three decades, Charles Perry Construction Inc. has built a reputation for excellence, integrity, and trust. As one of Gainesville's leading construction firms, Perry Construction has built many important structures in Gainesville.

■ Charles Perry Construction, Inc.'s partners Charles R. Perry and Breck A. Weingart.

Among them are the Alachua County courthouse, Florida Farm Bureau, Alachua County Library headquarters, Hospice House, Shands at AGH's Heart Center, emergency rooms at Shands at AGH and North Florida Regional Medical Center, the Atrium retirement community, Union Street Station in downtown Gainesville, numerous buildings at the University of Florida and Santa Fe Community College, and Nordstrom's distribution center. Add to that banks, prisons, churches, manufacturing facilities, multi-family homes, and athletic facilities. Perry has built them all.

Through a variety of delivery systems such as design build, construction management, and general contracting, Perry Construction's 100-plus team works with owners and managers to create quality projects, delivered on time and within budget.

"We are not a construction broker, but typically do concrete, carpentry, and general trades work with our own crews, which helps us maintain better control in terms of quality, standards, and schedules," says Breck A. Weingart, vice president.

Founded in 1968 by Charles R. Perry, Perry Construction has built long-term relationships not only with its customers but also with its valued employees.

"We're proud of the expertise represented on our staff," says Charles R. Perry, president. "Some Perry employees have been with the company 30 years. The dozen project managers and 18 superintendents have 650-plus years of experience. These folks take pride in their work and responsibility for their decisions," says Perry. "We work in concert, with mutual appreciation and respect being the hallmark of our team," he adds.

Perry Construction is committed to excellence in safety performance. Every team member works with management to eliminate accidents, resulting in a 50 percent reduction in overall accidents since 1992. In 1997 and 1999, Perry Construction worked the entire year without a lost-time accident—putting Perry Construction's injury rate well below the national average for the industry.

One of Gainesville's leading community contributors, Perry Construction has been involved with United Way, American Cancer Society, Junior Achievement, Boys and Girls Club, Hospice House, House of Hope, the Ronald McDonald House, Boy Scouts, Children's Miracle Network, Florida Museum of Natural History, University of Florida Bull Gators, Greater Gainesville Area Association for Technical Training, and the Gainesville Builders Association.

In 1998 Gainesville's Council for Economic Outreach recognized Perry Construction as Alachua County Corporate Citizen of the Year. Charles Perry was the named distinguished builder of the year in 1983. ■

■ 1329 Building.

ALLAN SPEAR CONSTRUCTION COMPANY _____

Whether it is a concrete foundation or intricate masonry work involving brick, stone, or glass block, the craftsmen at Allan Spear Construction Company have been involved in building many of Gainesville's most prominent structures.

■ Brick home built in the Gainesville Golf & Country Club.

The Spear Company employs 75 to 80, with numbers ranging to 250 during peak construction periods. "We've striven in the past 10 years to develop a core of competent foremen that we are real proud of," says Spear. "They've given us the ability to grow in size and complexity of jobs we can undertake."

One of the company's most important initiatives is in the area of safety. A full-time safety director handles all safety issues, including compliance with federal, state, and local safety ordinances and supervision of all employee training. "Safety is our number one priority," says Spear. "We want all our foremen, forklift operators, and scaffold workers to be well trained on the latest industrial equipment, so they will know how to operate safely at all times," he says.

With headquarters located in Gainesville, the firm maintains construction offices on the site of projects that last a year or more.

Allan Spear Construction Company is a distributor for Increte Systems, a stamped concrete product used in walkways, patios, driveways, and entrance areas.

Spear is president of the local masonry association, and the firm is a member of the Gainesville Area Chamber of Commerce, the Safety Council, and the Gainesville Builders Association. ■

"We've been here a long time, and we stand behind our work," says President Allan Spear III, who bought the business in 1993 from an uncle. He now runs the firm along with George Kusky, an employee of more than 26 years, who joined the firm as partner and vice president in 1991.

Allan Spear Construction Company began in 1955 as Doug Bishop Masonry. When Bishop decided to get out of the business, "my grandfather bought him out," says Spear. Since that time, Spear has expanded the business five-fold. To maintain growth the company looks nationwide to bid selected projects, and to date has landed jobs from Vero Beach to Georgia, while still maintaining steady growth within a two-hour radius of Gainesville.

"We handle both residential and commercial projects," says Spear. Some of the more notable masonry projects in the Gainesville area include: Lawton Chiles Elementary School, Kanapaha Middle School, Bellamy Grand Apartments, Cox Communications, Dollar General Distribution Warehouse, Stephen Foster Elementary School, SunTrust Bank, both University of Florida Foundation buildings, SouthWest Recreation Expansion, Reitz Union Expansion, Commerce Building, Oaks Square Mall, Tower Hill Office Complex, Physical Therapy Building at Shands, Oakview Middle School, Alltel Building, and UF's Alfred E. Ring Tennis Facility, a project that involved an intricate brick pattern called diagonal Flemish bond. "We're really proud of that project and its use of two different brick patterns," says Spear.

■ Diagonal Flemish brickwork on the Alfred E. Ring Tennis Pavilion on the University of Florida campus.

M. M. Parrish Construction Company

*W*hen Mercer Moorman Parrish Jr. built his first home in Gainesville, Florida, in 1940, he never dreamed what his company would become. Today with 200 employees and offices in Gainesville, Winter Haven, and Perry, Georgia, M. M. Parrish Construction Company, Inc., serves commercial, industrial, and institutional clients throughout Florida and Georgia and has an annual volume in excess of $60 million.

■ University of Florida, Academic Advisement.

A full-service construction company, M. M. Parrish provides construction management, design/build, and conventional general contracting services and retains excellent self-perform capabilities in concrete and carpentry work.

"We are very proud of our history, reputation, and the capabilities of the fine people on our staff," says Michael Walsh, president. "Our people are really what make us the company we are today," he says. Many Parrish employees have worked for the firm more than 20 years.

In addition to the skilled craftsmen and professionals who work on the Parrish team, Walsh sites leadership that has helped the firm grow and prosper. Past presidents include Parrish, Harris Nobles, and Joel Buzbee—people who have helped the company build important and long-lasting relationships with its clients, architects, sub contractors, and suppliers.

M. M. Parrish Construction has left a sizeable imprint on the community's landscape. Projects have included the south end zone, sky boxes, and concrete work for the north end zone at the University of Florida's (UF) Florida Field, UF's Academic Advisement Center, Criser Hall at UF, Sid Martin Biotechnology Research and

Development Facility at Progress Center, Kanapaha Middle School, Children's Medical Services Center, Talbot Elementary School, and Wiles Elementary School.

In response to a need for Florida and Georgia school districts to replace portable buildings with permanent classrooms, M. M. Parrish developed "The Parrish Classroom Solution," an innovative concrete classroom building that can be built quickly and economically. In addition to speed and economy, superior wind resistance, thermal and acoustical properties, fire ratings, and termite resistance are trademarks of the Parrish Classroom Solution.

While innovation and relationships are key to the success of the company, another important factor has been safety. "Our top priority on every project is safety," says Walsh.

Walsh credits the company's dependability for keeping customers coming back. "We've worked hard to be known as a company with integrity, that can be depended upon to get the job done on time and to a high degree of quality. Very few companies our size have principals of the firm on each job site on a regular basis," he says. Fred Nobles, chief executive officer, and Lloyd Whann, executive vice president, oversee all fieldwork.

A good neighbor and corporate citizen, M. M. Parrish is active in Rotary and supports many community interests including the House of Hope, Boys and Girls Club of Alachua County, Babe Ruth Baseball, and Habitat for Humanity. ■

■ University of Florida, Ben Hill Griffin Stadium.

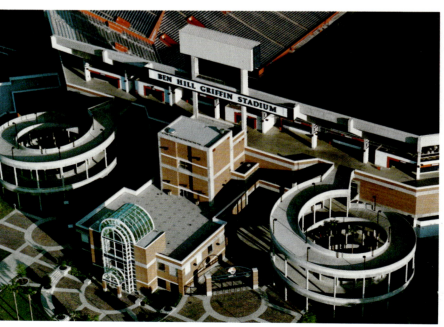

PPI Construction Management ————————

Named for the second consecutive year to the list of Florida's 100 fastest growing companies, PPI Construction Management has developed a successful business model by focusing on the core principals of knowledge, integrity, and placing the needs of clients first. Founding partner, Charles Perry Construction has been a fixture in the construction industry in Florida since the 1960s.

■ Alachua County Health Department.

PPI continues in this tradition of excellence by providing an impressive array of services to educational, health-care, institutional, criminal justice, and governmental markets throughout Florida and the Southeast.

"Our team's record of performance in meeting our clients' objectives is the cornerstone of our firm's reputation," said PPI President John V. Carlson. "We are particularly proud of our commitment to quality and our history of building relationships based on experience, value, and trust." With corporate headquarters in Gainesville and an office in Orlando, PPI has completed more than 150 projects throughout Central and North Central Florida in the last five years.

In the Gainesville area, PPI has provided Construction Management services on the new Alachua County Courthouse, the Alachua County Health Department, Shands Hospital at Starke, Santa Fe Community College Library, and many projects at the University of Florida (UF), including: new skybox additions to the Ben Hill Griffin Stadium, the Health Professions Nursing and Pharmacy Complex, the Gator Basketball Practice Facility, the Engineering Research Facility for Particle Science, Smathers Library Renovations, and Oak Hammock at UF, a continuing care retirement community. PPI constructed Lawton Chiles Elementary School and K-12 schools in seven other counties.

In addition to conventional building systems, PPI has a well-established Corrections Group that is involved in the manufacture of pre-cast modular prison detention cells. PPI has provided services for correctional facilities to local, state, and private clients on a national basis and has recently received its first international assignment providing consulting services for the development of private prisons in Curitiba, Brazil.

"PPI has a strong commitment to developing minority leadership in the construction industry," said Carlson. PPI not only actively seeks out and engages with minority contractors, but also sponsors workshops for minority businesses in conjunction with the State Department of Management Services and the University of Florida. The firm was recently recognized for its efforts by the UF Division of Small Business and Vendor Diversity Relations group.

Although active throughout the state, PPI has not forgotten its local roots. The firm is actively involved with the United Way, March of Dimes, WUFT-TV, the House of Hope, Alachua County Schools Foundation, Ronald McDonald House, Children's Museum of the South, Hospice, Children's Miracle Network, and a host of other community service groups. ■

■ University of Florida, Engineering Research for Particle Science.

SCHERER CONSTRUCTION & ENGINEERING, LLC

Specializing in light commercial projects up to $3.5 million in size, Scherer Construction & Engineering, LLC's Gainesville office is one of five offices strategically located throughout the Southeast. Founded in St. Petersburg, Florida, in 1984 by Clark H. Scherer III, chief executive officer, Scherer Construction & Engineering employs 96 people, with 19 located in Gainesville. Other offices are located in St. Petersburg, Orlando, Macon, and Atlanta.

■ Design/Build 22,000-square-foot commercial tire and full-service truck facility located off of I-75.

"The company was founded using the design/build concept, so owners can contract for architecture, construction management, and engineering with one firm at one time," said Doug Wilcox, president of Scherer Construction & Engineering of North Florida, located in Gainesville. "This makes it much easier for owners to oversee projects from conception to completion." Scherer completes its design/build projects with its own staff architect and civil/structural engineer. "There is one contact with sole responsibility and sole liability," said Wilcox. This process can save four to six months on a typical commercial project. In addition to design/build, Scherer also is a developer on some projects.

Wilcox joined the firm in 1986 as a building construction student. After graduation from the University of Florida, he stayed with the firm and became its president in 1992. He is a state-certified general contractor, roofing contractor, and underground utility contractor.

The North Florida office of Scherer Construction has constructed eight Eckerd Drug Stores, eight projects for Campus USA Credit Union, Walgreen's, several projects for the Salvation Army, Texas Roadhouse Restaurant, 15 projects for Rite Aid Drugs, Goodyear Commercial Truck Service Facility, La-Z-Boy Furniture, Archer Road Carwash, Barnes & Noble Bookstore, Schlotsky's Deli, several dentist offices, and numerous commercial distribution facilities.

Wilcox is proud of the company's low employee turnover. "After people come on board, they tend to stay for a long time," said Wilcox. "We have good people that work for us—people that take pride in their workmanship." In addition to low turnover, Wilcox cites Scherer's dedication to cutting-edge technology as another advantage. The firm's Web site is www.designbuild.com. "Using the latest technology, we are able to deliver a quality project with aggressive schedules on time," he said. "We're really from the old school. We do what we say we are going to do."

That dedication to customer service has had impressive results. Ninety percent of the firm's business comes from repeat customers. "We make sure our customers are satisfied with our service," said Wilcox. "We try to get everything right from the beginning, but we will do what it takes to correct or solve any problems," he said.

In the community, Scherer Construction & Engineering is involved with the YMCA, the Gainesville Area Chamber of Commerce, Northwood Commercial Park Owners Association, the Gainesville Builders Association, and Littlewood Elementary School. ■

■ Popular 3,060-square-foot restaurant on SW 34 Street.

TOWN OF TIOGA

Enter the Town of Tioga and you will witness something very special in the making. What was once merely a vision has become one of the most beautiful expressions of community development in Florida.

■ At the heart of the recreation corridor is the Meeting Hall and Community Pool with Cabana.

Nestled among giant oaks on the site of a turn of the century settlement, the Town of Tioga features amenities such as an attractive community pool, architecturally impressive meeting hall, basketball and tennis courts, beach volleyball, and a secured, modern tot-lot for children's play.

The vision of developers Miguel and Luis Diaz, Tioga continues to unfold as the community matures. Of course, the highlight of Tioga is its homes.

"If there is such a thing as a home that inspires the soul and imagination, it is found here," said Deborah Minck, real estate broker and director of sales for the community. "Each new home is an extension of the builders' ability to translate visual desire into practical function."

Homes are built with the latest in energy efficiency standards and the highest quality in home construction. Prices range from $170,000 to $500,000. The Town of Tioga's team of builders, architects, and interior designers work together to build homes that reflect a first-class southern lifestyle. "Those fortunate enough to establish themselves here will experience daily the beauty of nature and elegant design," Minck says.

The Town of Tioga has been called "a jewel of Alachua County" and has been recognized as a premier community locally, statewide, and nationally. In 1998, the Town of Tioga received the 1998 ENVY Award for "Best Community in Florida" from the Florida Association of Realtors. Tioga was also given the Gold Award for "Best Overall Community of the Millennium" presented by the Keep Alachua County Beautiful Foundation.

Nationally, Tioga won the Gold Award for 2001 "Best in American Living Smart Growth Community Award" from the National Association of Home Builders and *Professional Builders Magazine*. This award is the nation's foremost residential design competition and pays tribute to those who efficiently and innovatively produce communities with residential, commercial, and recreational uses while providing open green space and protecting environmentally sensitive areas.

With the proven integrity and commitment to excellence of Miguel and Luis Diaz and their team of professionals, the Town of Tioga will continue to be recognized for state-of-the-art design, smart growth, and traditional values.

The Town of Tioga is a community that continues to honor the land, focus on diversity of classic architectural style, and feature carefully planned alleyways, common areas, sidewalks, and bike lanes, encouraging greater pedestrian activity and neighborhood cohesiveness.

Tioga's hospitality and inviting nature make it a must-stop for those searching for their dream home or simply looking for a nice place for a Sunday drive. ■

■ Tioga's Esplanade invites young and old alike to stroll in the shade of its majestic oaks.

ENTERPRISE INDEX

Allan Spear Construction Company
2225 Northwest 66th Court
Gainesville, Florida 32653
Phone: 352-337-0773
Fax: 352-337-0788
E-mail: spearco@bellsouth.net
Page 153

AvMed Health Plan
PO Box 749
Gainesville, Florida 32602-0749
Phone: 352-372-8400
Fax: 352-337-8745
E-mail: members@avmed.org
www.avmed.org
Page 112

Barr Systems, Inc.
4500 Northwest 27th Avenue
Gainesville, Florida 32606-7031
Phone: 352-491-3100
Fax: 352-491-3141
E-mail: sales@barrsystems.com
www.barrsystems.com
Page 128

Cabot Lodge
3726 Southwest 40th Boulevard
Gainesville, Florida 32608
Phone: 352-375-2400
Toll-free: 800-843-8735
Fax: 352-335-2321
E-mail: gnvcl.sales@mmicmail.com
www.cabotlodge.com
Page 111

Campus USA Credit Union
2511 Northwest 41st Street
PO Box 147029
Gainesville, Florida 32606
Phone: 352-335-9090
Fax: 352-335-1094
E-mail: info@campuscu.com
www.campuscu.com
Pages 138-139

Charles Perry Construction Inc.
2500 Northeast 18th Terrace
Gainesville, Florida 32609
Phone: 352-378-1488
Fax: 352-378-0995
Page 152

Compass Bank
2814 Southwest 34th Street
Gainesville, Florida 32608
Phone: 352-367-5000
Fax: 352-367-5063
www.CompassWeb.com
Page 147

Dell Graham, Attorneys at Law
203 Northeast 1st Street
Gainesville, Florida 32601
Phone: 352-372-4381
Fax: 352-376-7415
E-mail: firm@dellgraham.com
www.dellgraham.com
Page 146

Exactech
2320 Northwest 66th Court
Gainesville, Florida 32653
Phone: 352-377-1140
www.exac.com
Pages 126-127

Gainesville Area Chamber of Commerce
300 East University Avenue
Gainesville, Florida 32602
Phone: 352-334-7100
Fax: 352-334-7141
E-mail: info@gainesvillechamber.com
www.gainesvillechamber.com
Pages 136-137

Gainesville Regional Utilities
PO Box 147117
MS #A134
Gainesville, Florida 32614-7117
Phone: 352-334-3400
Fax: 352-334-2277
E-mail: gru@gru.com
www.gru.com
Pages 116-117

Gillen Broadcasting
7120 Southwest 24th Avenue
Gainesville, Florida 32607
Phone: 352-331-2200
Fax: 352-331-0401
E-mail: kiss1053@aol.com
www.kiss1053.com
Pages 118-119

Ixion Biotechnology, Inc.
13709 Progress Boulevard
Box 13
Alachua, Florida 32615
Phone: 386-418-1428
Fax: 386-418-1583
E-mail: info@ixion-biotech.com
www.ixion-biotech.com
Page 132

Legacy at Fort Clarke
1505 Fort Clarke Boulevard
Gainesville, Florida 32606
Phone: 352-331-9322
Fax: 352-331-9303
E-mail: spchip@aol.com
www.rent.net/direct/legacyatfortclarke
Pages 150-151

Medical Device Technologies, Inc.
3600 Southwest 47th Avenue
Gainesville, Florida 32608
Phone: 352-338-0440
Fax: 352-338-0662
www.mdtech.com
Page 130

M. M. Parrish Construction Company
3455 Southwest 42nd Avenue
Gainesville, Florida 32608
Phone: 352-378-1571
Fax: 352-377-0669
E-mail: mikew@parrishconstruction.com
www.parrishconstruction.com
Page 154

Moltech Power Systems
12801 US Highway 441 North
Alachua, Florida 32615
Phone: 386-462-3911
Fax: 386-462-4726
www.moltech.com
Page 121

Nationwide Insurance
3300 Williston Road
Gainesville, Florida 32608
Phone: 352-377-8500
www.nationwide.com
Pages 142-143

PPI Construction Management
8200 Northwest 15th Place
Gainesville, Florida 32606
Phone: 352-375-2006
Fax: 352-376-7100
E-mail: jrc@perry-parrish.com
www.perry-parrish.com
Page 155

Residence Inn by Marriott
4001 Southwest 13th Street
Gainesville, Florida 32608
Phone: 352-371-2101
Fax: 352-377-2247
Page 110

Regeneration Technologies, Inc.
Two Innovation Drive
Alachua, Florida 32615
Phone: 904-418-8888
Fax: 904-418-0342
www.regenerationtechnologies.com
Page 129

Santa Fe Community College
3000 Northwest 83rd Street
Gainesville, Florida 32606
Phone: 352-395-5000
Fax: 352-395-5581
E-mail: information@santafe.cc.fl.us
www.santafe.cc.fl.us
Pages 108-109

Scherer Construction & Engineering, LLC
2501 Northwest 66th Court
Gainesville, Florida 32653
Phone: 352-371-1417
Fax: 352-338-1018
E-mail: dougwilcox@designbuild.com
www.designbuild.com
Page 156

Shands HealthCare
PO Box 100326
1600 Southwest Archer Road
Gainesville, Florida 32610-0326
Phone: 352-265-0664
Fax: 352-265-0321
E-mail: tubbml@shands.ufl.edu
www.shands.org
Pages 100-103

Technology Enterprise Center of Gainesville/Alachua County
2153 Hawthorne Road
Gainesville, Florida 32641
Phone: 352-393-6000
www.gtecflorida.com
Pages 144-145

Tower Hill Insurance Group
7201 Northwest 11th Place
Gainesville, Florida 32605
Phone: 352-332-8800
Fax: 352-332-9999
www.towerhillinsurance.com
Pages 140-141

Town of Tioga
205 Southwest 131st Street
Tioga, Florida 32669
Toll-free: 866-332-3009
Fax: 352-333-3008
E-mail: deborah@townoftioga.com
www.townoftioga.com
Page 157

Tower Communications, Inc.
1830 Northeast 2nd Street
Gainesville, Florida 32609
Toll-free: 800-395-5196
Fax: 352-371-9523
E-mail: info@callust.com
www.callust.com
Page 122

University of Florida
PO Box 113156
207 Tigert
Gainesville, Florida 32611
Phone: 352-846-3903
Fax: 352-846-3908
E-mail: gfbaker@ufl.edu
www.ufl.edu
Pages 104-107

University of Florida's
Sid Martin Biotechnology Development Incubator
12085 Research Drive
Alachua, Florida 32615
Phone: 386-462-0880
Fax: 386-462-0875
E-mail: patti@biotech.ufl.edu
www.biotech.ufl.org
Page 131

U.S. Cellular
6020 Northwest 4th Place
Gainesville, Florida 32607
Fax: 352-665-4353
E-mail: deirdre.racanelli@uscellular.com
www.uscellular.com
Page 120

PHOTO INDEX